STARTING TO COLLECT SERIES

ANTIQUE JEWELLERY

John Benjamin

STARTING TO COLLECT SERIES

ANTIQUE JEWELLERY

John Benjamin

ANTIQUE COLLECTORS' CLUB

Frontispiece: Italian micromosaic and gold necklace and cross, c.1860-1870. S.J. Phillips

Origination by the Antique Collectors' Club Ltd., Woodbridge, Suffolk, England
Printed and bound in Spain

THE ANTIQUE COLLECTORS' CLUB

Formed in 1966, the Antique Collectors' Club is now a world-renowned publisher of top quality books for the collector. It also publishes the only independently-run monthly antiques magazine, *Antique Collecting*, which rose quickly from humble beginnings to a network of worldwide subscribers.

The magazine, whose motto is *For Collectors-By Collectors-About Collecting*, is aimed at collectors interested in widening their knowledge of antiques both by increasing their awareness of quality and by discussion of the factors influencing prices.

Subscription to Antique Collecting is open to anyone interested in antiques and subscribers receive ten issues a year. Well-illustrated articles deal with practical aspects of collecting and provide numerous tips on prices, features of value, investment potential, fakes and forgeries. Offers of related books at special reduced prices are also available only to subscribers.

In response to the enormous demand for information on 'what to pay', ACC introduced in 1968 the famous price guide series. The first title, *The Price Guide to Antique Furniture* (since renamed *British Antique Furniture: Price Guide and Reasons for Values*), is still in constant demand. Since those pioneering days, ACC has gone from strength to strength, publishing many of today's standard works of reference on all things antique and collectable, from *Tiaras* to *20th Century Ceramic Designers in Britain*.

Not only has ACC continued to cater strongly for its original audience, it has also branched out to produce excellent titles on many subjects including art reference, architecture, garden design, gardens, and textiles. All ACC's publications are available through bookshops worldwide and a catalogue is available free of charge from the addresses below.

For further information please contact:

ANTIQUE COLLECTORS' CLUB

www.antique-acc.com

Sandy Lane, Old Martlesham
Woodbridge, Suffolk IP12 4SD, UK
Tel: 01394 389950 Fax: 01394 389999
Email: info@antique-acc.com
——————— or ———————
Market Street Industrial Park
Wappingers' Falls, NY 12590, USA
Tel: 845 297 0003 Fax: 845 297 0068
Email: info@antiquecc.com

FOR P.C.K. – WITH LOVE

ACKNOWLEDGEMENTS

The vast majority of the photographs which appear in this book have been sourced from leading London jewellery shops, long-established members of the trade, museums and auction houses. I am indeed indebted to all my colleagues in the business for their kindness in allowing their stock, and many personal items, to be removed and photographed.

I should particularly like to thank Mr. Jonathan Norton and his colleagues at S.J. Phillips, not only for supplying numerous transparencies but also for the use of the firm's premises for filming. My particular thanks to Mr. Paul Greer at Bentley & Skinner; Mr. Duncan Semmens at Hancocks & Co. Ltd.; Miss Sandra Cronan; Mr. Kieran McCarthy at Wartski Jewellers Ltd. and John Jesse and Gateway Studio Photographers (who supplied many of the images of Arts and Crafts jewellery).

I am especially grateful to my former colleague at Phillips Auctioneers, Mr. Keith Penton, for his kindness and generosity and Mr. Paul Viney of Woolley and Wallis for the use of many essential photographs.

The following dealers at Grays Antique Market in Davies Street, London, lent items from their stock: Brian and Lynn Holmes, Sylvie Spectrum, Shapiro & Co., Satoe, RBR Group, Michael Longmore, John Joseph and Wimpole Antiques.

The Museum of London and Waddesdon Manor supplied important historical images of Renaissance, 17th century and memento mori jewellery.

I should also like to extend my thanks to Mrs. Pat Novissimo, Mrs. Diana Foley, James and Elizabeth Gosling, Ms. Madeleine Popper, Ms. Ginny Redington Dawes, Miss Linda Morgan, Mrs. Etienne Brown, Mrs. Vicky Waller, Mrs. Sylvia Quenet-Chute and my photographer Mr. Don Wood for his consummate skill and professionalism.

Finally I should like to say thank you to my wife Patricia who, apart from typing the copy, gave me unwavering encouragement in the development of the book.

CONTENTS

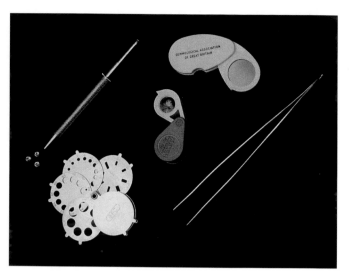

Basic tools of the trade: a Zeiss 10x lens, a gauge for measuring diamonds, tweezers, stone grips and a Chelsea colour filter to help in the identification and differentiation of gems such as emerald, aquamarine and synthetic spinel.

A Moe diamond weight gauge and a Leveridge millimetre gauge. Both instruments are simple to use and are invaluable for the assessment of the weights and dimensions of diamonds and gemstones.

INTRODUCTION

I began my career in the jewellery trade in 1972 when, after leaving school, I started work as an apprentice at Cameo Corner, an antique jewellers in Bloomsbury, London. The shop was situated some fifty yards from the gates of the British Museum and was just a stone's throw from University College, Lincoln's Inn and Covent Garden. The area was jam-packed with antiquarian booksellers, antique shops, academics who daily occupied the Reading Room at the Museum, artists, writers and a fair number of eccentrics who seemed to gravitate towards what was then a rather bohemian area of London. It was certainly the ideal environment for a young and keen junior shop assistant to learn about such a strongly aesthetic subject as antique jewellery.

Cameo Corner was established in the 1920s by Mosheh Oved, a Polish Jew who had started with next to nothing – although by the time of his death in 1953 the shop could boast a list of celebrated and significant clients including the sculptor Jacob Epstein, several foreign princesses and our own Queen Mary (who enjoyed the exclusive use of her own armchair). The shop specialised in a broad spectrum of rare and beautiful jewels and gems from Ancient Rome to Victorian England and, naturally, we always kept a large stock of cameos mounted into rings, brooches or even complete sets in their original fitted cases. One cabinet contained a group of Renaissance enamels and another an assortment of Italian Revivalist collars and bracelets jostling with Regency amethyst and garnet diadems. Our incomparable collection of Greek and Roman gold torcs and ancient artefacts was lodged in a safe at the back of the shop. In 1974 much of this irreplaceable stock disappeared in an armed robbery, never to be seen again.

I believe that there are four principal differences between the jewellery industry in the 1970s and that of today. Firstly, *availability*. In those days, Victorian gold – particularly low carat pendants and bangles –

was so abundant that it sold for negligibly more than scrap. Today, a gold collar with locket or a pair of revivalist teardrop earrings are scarce, highly sought and expensive.

Secondly, *value*. Whatever the item, be it a Giuliano pendant, a piece of Imperial jade or a Victorian silver sweetheart brooch, the price has shot up reflecting rarity, collectability and demand. How many times have I heard a veteran dealer bemoan the fact that the pretty Belle Epoque ring which has just cost him £5,000 could be bought for £250 thirty years ago!

Thirdly, *fashion*. In much the same way that unfashionable 'estate' jewels, diamonds and old gems were routinely broken up for re-cutting and re-setting, so much period jewellery has undergone several phases of reassessment, often experiencing surges and losses in popularity and associated value. A few years ago, Post War 'Retro' jewellery was proving difficult to sell and currently Victorian diamond flower sprays are in low demand. No doubt in ten years' time 9 carat gold charm bracelets will be the ultimate in chic. Now they sell at auction for little more than scrap.

Fourthly, *knowledge*. This factor has had an enormous impact upon how we understand and value jewellery today. When I first joined the business very few people knew about Mughal jewellery, fancy diamonds or 'obscure' 19th century

goldsmiths like Jules and Louis Wiese. Today erudite books and auction house catalogues supply lengthy descriptions and biographies accompanied by state of the art colour photographs. Lectures, courses and workshops are held all over the world by acknowledged specialists and exhibitions display rare and neglected pieces previously locked away, undiscovered, for generations. Together with popular television programmes like the *Antiques Roadshow* and the accessibility of the Internet, there has never been a time when information about jewellery has been so universally available.

The aim of *Starting to Collect Antique Jewellery* is to provide the sort of fundamental information which will enable the collector, student and enthusiast to recognise and identify many of the varieties of antique jewellery readily available on the market today. The scope of the book embraces early times to Art Deco and several important single topics such as gemstones, mourning jewellery, revivalist jewellery and paste are explored, as well as practical information on repairs and valuations. *Starting to Collect Antique Jewellery* is, however, *not* a price guide. In my opinion the best method of understanding how goods are valued – and constructed – is to adopt the 'hands on' approach and spend time inspecting jewellery at specialist auctions in the U.K. and overseas.

Interior of Cameo Corner, 26 Museum Street, London. Note the cabinets on the right filled from top to bottom with antique parures.

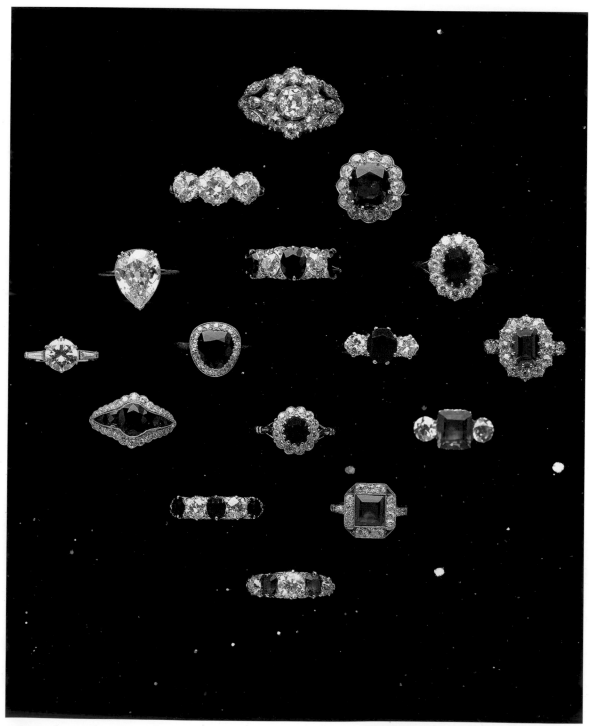

A group of diamond, sapphire, ruby and emerald rings illustrating a broad range of designs from the Regency period to today.

Bentley & Skinner

CHAPTER 1

GEMMOLOGY AND GEMS IN ANTIQUE JEWELLERY

Gemmology is the science of gemstones. In Britain a two year course in the theoretical and practical study of gemmology leads to an internationally recognised qualification: F.G.A. or Fellow of the Gemmological Association. The equivalent course in the U.S.A. results in the successful applicant achieving the status of Graduate Gemologist or G.G.

The fact that you are an F.G.A. will give you a visible advantage over unqualified competitors simply because you will have the knowledge and confidence of examining a piece of jewellery and being able to differentiate between any number of valuable gems and their less valuable or worthless counterparts. Once qualified, an F.G.A. can choose to go on and take a further year's Diploma course in the study and examination of diamonds (D.G.A.).

In the world of gemstones, confusion frequently reigns supreme. Antique jewellery compounds the problem perfectly since many old gems which appear to be one thing are found to be something quite different. Here are some examples. A late Victorian diamond brooch with a 'coral' drop is found to be a rare and costly pink conch pearl. A Regency necklace of graduated pink 'topaz' is actually foil-back rock crystals worth a quarter of the price. An aquamarine ring priced at £2,000 is found on testing to be man-made synthetic blue spinel worth £50 and a 1950s gold brooch set with a 'fine harlequin black opal' is actually an opal triplet, a 'sandwich' of modest opal and crystal. Probably one of the most notorious of these man-made stones masquerading as the real thing is synthetic corundum. Possessing the ability of changing colour in natural or artificial light, these near-valueless gems are sold on as Alexandrite, a highly sought and extremely expensive variety of chrysoberyl. It is indeed very easy to come unstuck where gems are concerned and, therefore, a basic knowledge of gemstones and their simulants can help to make – or save – you thousands of pounds.

Gemstones are invariably divided into several distinct categories based upon a variety of factors of which beauty, durability, rarity and value are the dominant characteristics dictating in which 'column' the gem tends to be listed. These categories are highly subjective and the cause of endless debate. Take jade as an example. An Imperial jade bead necklace can sell internationally for millions of dollars whilst a crude nephrite jade modern carving may be worth less than £50. Similarly, a 19th century gilt metal and deep red Bohemian garnet star brooch may fetch only £75 whilst the rare green demantoid garnet can achieve as much as £6,000 *per carat* at auction.

The following tables are a personal – and by no means exhaustive – categorisation, chosen within the context of identifying those gems and materials most commonly encountered in antique jewellery.

Table One: Precious Stones
Diamond
Corundum (Ruby and Sapphire)
Emerald
Precious Black Opal
Imperial Jadeite
Alexandrite

Table Two: Semi-Precious Stones

Amethyst	Peridot
Aquamarine	Rock Crystal
Chrysoberyl	Spinel
Citrine	Topaz
Garnet	Tourmaline
Moonstone	Turquoise
Opal	Zircon

Table Three: Ornamental Hardstones

Agate	Labradorite
Bloodstone	Lapis Lazuli
Chalcedony	Malachite
Chrysoprase	Nephrite Jade
Cornelian	Non-precious jadeite
Fluorspar	Onyx and Sardonyx
Jasper	Rose quartz

Table Four: Organic Materials

Pearl
Amber
Coral
Ivory
Jet
Shell
Tortoiseshell

PRECIOUS STONES

DIAMOND

Diamond is carbon in its purest state. Appropriately enough, its name is taken from the Ancient Greek word *Adamas* meaning 'unconquerable.' Diamond is the stuff of legends, intrigue, romance, betrayal and greed. Of all gems, it fulfils the necessary criteria for being considered a truly precious stone. It is the

'D Flawless' marquise-shaped brilliant-cut diamond. The finest colour and clarity on the market.

hardest and most durable natural substance on earth. Its beauty is arguably unsurpassed. It is phenomenally difficult to mine and extract and is unrivalled in value.

Diamonds are assessed using four basic factors – the so-called '4 Cs' – and each of these factors will play a critical role when calculating the value of any given stone.

(i) *Colour.* The vast majority of diamonds found in jewellery are almost colourless or exhibit a slight tint of yellow. The degree of yellow is actually extremely subtle and difficult to judge, especially when comparing two stones at the 'colourless' or top end of the range. The jewellery industry uses an alphabetical scale to differentiate colour where 'D' is totally colourless and 'Z' is visibly yellow, so telling the difference between, say, a G colour and an H colour diamond requires skill and experience. Many jewellers and diamond merchants own sets of specimen diamonds of a known colour so they can compare two stones and make a confident judgement. The difference in price between diamonds which *appear* identical may actually be several thousands of dollars per carat.

A diamond may frequently be such a good colour that it requires certification at one of the world's internationally recognised laboratories. This is particularly relevant when dealing with larger stones or antique diamonds where significant numbers of crystals are celebrated for their exceptional lack of colour – and fine clarity.

(ii) *Clarity.* It is extremely rare to find a diamond which is totally free of impurities or 'internally flawless.' The impurities in a diamond are known as *inclusions* and range from black spots of carbon to white crystals, cracks, fractures, stress lines and surface imperfections which must all be visible under 10x magnification. As with colour, an internationally recognised scale of clarity has been adopted ranging from Internally Flawless (IF) to Third Piqué (I3). Diamonds worse than piqué are usually referred to as spotted and are, frankly, so poor as to render them unsuitable for setting in jewellery. Diamonds which are so heavily flawed that they appear almost opaque are set aside for use in the industrial sector, where their supreme hardness means they are eminently suitable for more robust tasks such as drill heads, grinding wheels and the optical industry.

(iii) *Cut* refers to the shape of a diamond and how it is polished. The most popular and, therefore, highest value shape for diamond is the round *brilliant,* consisting of fifty-eight perfectly proportioned facets to allow maximum brilliance. This is the so-called 'make' of the stone and a well-made diamond will command a considerable premium in price whilst a poorly made stone will in turn lose some of its value. Modern diamonds are cut into many diverse shapes with ever-increasing numbers of complicated facets. Popular traditional shapes include the rectangular emerald-cut, the marquise (boat or torpedo shape), the heart, the oval, the baguette (small emerald-cuts used extensively in jewellery from the 1930s), and the *briolette* (diamond faceted beads). Antique diamonds were often cut from crystals which came from long dried-up alluvial deposits in countries such as India and Brazil. These old stones retain a 'soft' purity and beauty which is often why antique diamond pieces are broken up for repolishing into modern stones – more valuable and desirable because of their historical origin than many stones from 'modern' mines.

(iv) *Carat* is the unit of weight for all diamonds and gemstones and is equal to one fifth of a gram. The word 'carat' is taken form the Greek *keration* or 'little horn.' It was discovered by pearl merchants in ancient times that the dried seeds of the carob tree were extremely reliable units of weight due to their uniformity of size; these seeds were contained in bean pods which closely resembled little horns and, thus, the name carat gained common usage. A diamond which, say, weighs three and a half carats is described as '3.50 carats' and one of half a carat as '0.50 carats'. The second decimal point is an important criterion when differentiating the weight of two diamonds of apparently similar size.

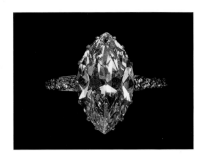

Marquise-shaped fancy vivid diamond ring c.1910. Such 'old-mine' fancy diamonds are rare and in high demand today.

Coloured Diamonds

The extraordinarily high price which is paid at international auction for fancy coloured diamonds is actually a relatively recent phenomenon. Certainly, prior to the 1970s, the beauty and rarity of a pink or blue diamond may have been recognised, but prices were nothing like as astronomic as they are today. In Victorian times coloured diamonds were collected as curiosities but 'white' diamonds were commercially more desirable and invariably dearer in price.

Diamonds are found in all colours of the rainbow, although the rarest is red. In 1987 a purplish-red diamond weighing 0.95 carats fetched $880,000 – $926,000 per carat – at auction. It is the purity and intensity of colour which determines its value; a yellow diamond graded as 'vivid' is far more expensive than a lighter yellow 'intense' diamond, whilst a 'greyish blue' diamond is far less desirable than, say, a 'deep blue' stone. This is why fancy diamonds are always sent to an international laboratory so their precise colour can be scientifically assessed. Generally speaking, brown is the least expensive fancy colour and black is surprisingly affordable in price, although the recent popularity of setting numerous small black diamonds in contrasting clusters with colourless diamonds has increased their popularity and value.

It is possible to find beautiful coloured diamonds in antique brooches and pendants. Invariably, these stones are removed from their settings for repolishing into modern, perfectly proportioned gems with enhanced value. An excellent method of collecting fancy coloured diamonds is to search for Victorian tiepins where it was reasonably common to set a single specimen stone into a simple claw setting of gold. These diamonds are usually too small to be of great commercial merit and it is perfectly possible to build up a reasonable spectrum of colours for a not unrealistic outlay.

Diamond Cutting Through History

Diamonds have been set into jewellery since Roman times and throughout history have been prized for all sorts of properties and powers including magical, medicinal and talismanic. In medieval times wearing diamonds could apparently prevent the plague and powdered diamond was reliably considered to be a potent poison. During the Middle Ages, and well into the 16th century, unpolished diamond crystals were set into gold rings and were used for writing messages on window panes. Known as 'pointed'

diamonds, these octahedral crystals were set with the point of the natural unpolished, four-sided pyramid above the top of the gold mount and possessed one unrivalled property – they never wore out.

The most basic method of faceting a diamond was the *table-cut* – quite simply an unpolished octahedral crystal with its top ground down into a square. Sometimes the opposing point of the crystal was also removed, creating a smaller facet at the back of the stone, known as the *culet*. The table-cut reigned supreme throughout the 16th and 17th centuries – unsurprising, considering the technical difficulties in polishing a diamond with the primitive tools available.

Diamond polishers in Amsterdam and Antwerp experimented with more complex methods of cutting as early as the 15th century and it was in Holland that a new style of faceting gradually emerged. Known as the *rose-cut,* the crown or top of the diamond was cut into a series of geometric triangular facets, whilst the pavilion, or bottom of the stone, was left flat. Rose diamonds became extremely popular throughout the 18th and 19th centuries, although they tend to appear rather grey in comparison with diamonds of more complex cut. They were invariably set in silver in tightly enclosed bands known as *collets*. They lent themselves beautifully to the many designs of

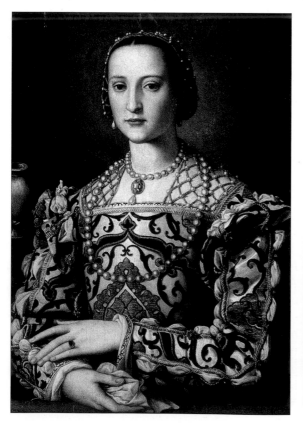

(Left) Splendid rose-cut diamond and old-mine cut diamond lyre brooch c.1800.
S.J. Phillips

(Far left) Eleonora di Toledo by Agnolo Bronzino, c.1545. The subject, wife of Cosimo I de Medici, is wearing a rope of magnificent pearls suspending a large table-cut diamond pendant with Baroque pearl drop.

Old mine brilliant cut diamond chandelier earrings with antique Indian briolette diamond drops c.1850.
Woolley & Wallis

jewellery fashionable during this period – aigrettes, collet rivières, girandole earrings and naturalistic cluster rings. Sometimes rose diamonds were backed with silver tinfoil to intensify their sparkle.

By the middle of the 18th century society was beginning to enjoy the benefits of increasing wealth. Socially, this prosperity meant that ladies and gentlemen of the nobility and a burgeoning middle class were keen to dress up and meet one another at balls, the theatre and at receptions held in their splendid new houses and country estates. Here they could show off to one another the latest gown from London and Paris complemented by ravishing tiaras, corsage jewels and chandelier earrings mounted with *brilliant-cut* diamonds – the new style of polishing which, for the first time, showed diamonds off to their best effect. A modern brilliant is composed of fifty-eight perfectly proportioned facets but antique brilliants are often rather ill-proportioned and cushion in shape. Nevertheless, the impact of a Georgian faceted diamond brooch worn in the twinkling light of chandeliers and candelabra was breathtaking and made the diamond the most desirable and valuable of all gemstones in the 'Age of the Faceted Stone.'

The discovery of diamond deposits in South Africa in the 1870s – notably at Kimberley and sub-sequently in South West Africa – led to hundreds of thousands of carats being brought into Britain and Western Europe. In a boom economy where a more prosperous society possessed the necessary dis-posable income to buy jewellery, most of the principal towns and cities in Britain boasted several family jewellers catering for the needs of the public. In the 1890s diamond jewellery could be fairly modest – simple cluster brooches, crescents, stars, line bangles and half-hoop rings selling for considerably less than £100 – or far grander, such as the Goldsmiths & Silversmiths Company selling diamond crowns and necklaces for well over £1,000. The underlying theme was *availability.* Diamonds were both affordable and plentiful; by the end of the 19th century it was possible to buy a rivière of graduated diamonds from one London supplier in no less than twenty-three different sizes.

Mass production inevitably led to improvement in diamond cutting and by the start of the 20th century the introduction of platinum revolutionised both jewellery design and the technical accomplishment of mounting stones with the minimum of setting visible. Diamond cutters experimented with many different shapes – baguettes, emerald-cuts, mar-quises and briolettes, to name but a few – and the brilliant evolved into the perfectly proportioned symmetrical round stone exhibiting the unique adamantine lustre so familiar to us today.

CORUNDUM

Corundum is an oxide of aluminium which has two distinct varieties – ruby and sapphire. Although ruby is only found in shades of pale pink to deep red, sapphire is found in an entire spectrum of colours.

RUBY

An extremely fine precious ruby will compete in price with the costliest of diamonds whilst a poor colour ruby filled with an abundance of flaws rendering it opaque may only be worth £25 a carat.

Late Victorian Burma ruby and diamond cluster ring. Wimpole Antiques

Fine Burma ruby and diamond clasp c.1900 on a later Oriental pearl necklace.

Rubies gained particular prominence and recognition during the Renaissance, when richly coloured specimens were brought into Western Europe along the Trade routes from the Orient and were set into magnificent pendants and stomachers with diamonds and pearls. The most important stones were mined in Burma (Myanmar) and the very best Burmese examples are described as *pigeon's blood*. These rubies are characteristically a deep rich red colour due to the presence of chromium and are rarely found in sizes above four carats. Other sources for ruby include Ceylon (Sri Lanka) which produces paler stones of pinkish tone, Siam (Thailand) where the rubies are invariably purplish-pink or brownish due to the existence of iron, also Africa, Afghanistan and Vietnam.

Ruby was an important gemstone in 18th and 19th century jewellery. Its versatility meant that it could be set into contrasting lines or clusters with diamonds, half pearls or exclusively in elaborately chased gold mounts. In the period of mass production at the end of the 19th century, rubies were routinely set with diamonds in crescents, floral sprays, hinged gold bangles and modest cluster rings. These stones were usually of cushion shape and the quality was quite variable, although fine 'old-mine' Burmese stones are highly prized today. As stone cutting techniques advanced, ruby was cut into several new and interesting shapes including square, calibré (baton) and triangular. A popular design in the 1920s and 1930s was the line bracelet, where a channel of square-cut rubies was set in articulated side-by-side formation in a gold or platinum mount.

Fabergé used rubies, indigenous to Russia, which were an ideal accompaniment to the objects of function popular with his wealthy and sophisticated clientele; thus, bell pushes, photograph frames, gold brooches and cigarette cases were set with rubies polished 'en cabochon' into domes. The cabochon was the only possible method of cutting suitable for exhibiting the distinctive six-pointed star effect known as *asterism*. Star rubies and star sapphires were mounted in architectural diamond settings during the Art Deco period and were particularly popular in the U.S.A. Star rubies are less common than star sapphires and sell for significant sums dependent upon their quality and size.

SAPPHIRE

Although we tend to think that sapphires are blue, they are actually found in many lovely colours, of which one in particular – the padparadscha – can be as rare and costly as some of the best blue examples.

The finest sapphires were mined in the Kashmir region of India and are a singular shade of warm, velvety blue. The Kashmir mines are now exhausted so antique stones are prized not just for their colour but their rarity. Burmese sapphires are also rare and expensive and are a deeper, clearer royal blue. The majority of good quality Victorian sapphires are, like ruby, of Burmese origin – a classic brooch might be designed as a crescent of graduated cushion-shaped Burma sapphires within a border of old-mine cut diamonds.

(Above) Ceylon sapphire emerald-cut single-stone ring c.1925.   Woolley & Wallis

(Above right) Late Victorian Burma sapphire and diamond cluster ring. Such strong royal blue sapphires were an ideal accompaniment for the kind of diamond jewellery popular at the time – half hoop bangles and rings, cluster earrings and closed crescent brooches.   Wimpole Antiques

Ceylon sapphires are considerably paler and less valuable than the Burmese variety. Sometimes called 'cornflower blue', they are quite easy to identify as they invariably contain needle-like inclusions called 'silk' which reflect the light in a rainbow-like effect. Ceylon sapphires were used in late Victorian fringe necklaces, aesthetic jewellery in which a subtle tone of colour was considered appropriate and Art Nouveau jewellery. These sapphires were frequently 'native-cut' meaning that they were both poorly proportioned and fashioned to exhibit the best direction of colour. It is worthwhile to examine a Ceylon sapphire through the side of the stone – it is sometimes totally colourless.

Other sources for blue sapphire include Siam (Thailand), Australia – where the stones are so deep a blue as to appear black – and Montana, where bright blue examples were often set in Edwardian pearl pendants. Other desirable colours include pink – where a deep shade of magenta is highly prized – purple, green, yellow and brown. Colourless or 'white' sapphires are often set in Eastern jewellery where they contrast with blue sapphires, citrines, zircons and low grade emeralds. They are modestly priced and difficult to confuse with valuable diamonds.

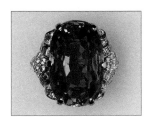

Unusually large cushion-shaped pink sapphire and diamond ring.

Padparadscha sapphires are hard to define. The trade describe their colour as 'peach' and certainly paler, cheaper examples do seem to have a 'peachy' tone. However, a really top grade padparadscha sapphire will exhibit a vibrant orangy-pink colour, a case of once seen never forgotten. Seldom encountered, a price of $10,000 per carat is not unknown.

Irregular polished rubies and sapphires were set in Roman gold rings and simple part-faceted examples appear in rings and brooches from the 13th and 14th centuries onwards. The rarity and quality of these jewels meant that their use was undoubtedly confined

to bishops and high churchmen, wealthy merchants and the nobility. During the 18th century rings were frequently foiled to enhance the colour and intensify the lustre of the sapphire (or any coloured gem come to that); this technique lapsed with the development of open-back settings, advances in stone cutting and the discovery of new mine deposits.

Sapphires were the perfect accompaniment to diamonds in the 19th century and, along with rubies, were extensively set in flower spray brooches, tiaras, earrings and endless half-hoop and floral cluster rings, universally popular from the 1880s onwards. Like ruby, sapphire was the ideal contrast to diamond in Art Deco platinum and white gold jewellery and after the First World War large, pale Ceylon sapphires were set in broad bracelets and bold yellow gold flower brooches enhanced by gems of unusual colour such as turquoise, zircon and rubies cut into rectangular batons.

EMERALD

It is an interesting paradox that although jewellery set with emeralds is reasonably common – especially in items manufactured after the Second World War – antique jewellery mounted with top quality 'old-mine' emeralds is extremely scarce.

Emerald is the green gem variety of beryl and has fairly widespread distribution. By far the most desirable antique stones originated in Colombia from the Chivor and Muzo mines. Their highly prized 'blue-green' colour is due to chromium and, internally, Colombian emeralds frequently contain characteristic 'three-phase inclusions' composed of a cavity filled with liquid, a gas bubble and a crystalline cube. Other sources of emerald include Russia (Siberia), Egypt – where mines can be traced as far back as Queen Cleopatra – Pakistan, Afghanistan and Africa. Emeralds from the Sandawana mines in Zimbabwe produce small stones of intense colour and fine clarity whilst less desirable pale and flawed stones were extracted from the old Habachtal mines in the Austrian Tyrol. Many of the semi-opaque, poor colour emeralds found in Renaissance revival jewellery at the end of the 19th century originated from this source.

As expensive as fine, old Colombian and Siberian

emeralds may be, indifferent emeralds containing an abundance of cracks, flaws and assorted imperfections are not. Poorer stones are often polished 'en cabochon' into domes which tends to mask internal defects better than the faceted varieties. Today emeralds are treated with caution by buyers because of the large number of stones on the market which have been 'improved' with oils, resins and artificial materials which strengthen colour and conceal defects. The problem has become so widespread that shops and auction houses publish disclaimers to protect themselves from legal dispute. Significant stones are thus sold at auction with an accompanying certificate stating natural, untreated colour and, ideally, country of origin.

Emerald was highly prized by the Ancient

Victorian Colombian emerald and diamond demi-parure c.1885. The necklace back is detachable allowing the front to be converted into an imposing tiara.

Egyptians and subsequently by the Spanish, who brought Colombian emeralds to India during the 16th century. Jewellery originating from this period tends to be of religious design; crosses, rosaries, crowns and vestment ornaments were invariably mounted with large table-cut emeralds which were frequently foiled to enhance their colour. Old Indian emeralds of 17th and 18th century origin were highly prized by the Mughal emperors, who set huge pebble-like stones in armbands, collars and head ornaments known as *sarpechs*. These stones were sometimes engraved with complicated calligraphy and flowers; a fine 217 carat inscribed example sold at auction in September 2001 for a hammer price of £1.4 million.

Emerald and diamond jewellery was highly prized by European aristocracy during the 18th and 19th centuries. Complete parures of necklace, earrings, corsage brooch and tiara were lavishly mounted with Indian and Colombian stones, set in gold collets within diamond and silver frames of sévigné (tied bow), cluster and floral drop design. During the early 19th century foil-back emeralds were set in highly elaborate cannetille work gold frames and the gem was popular in sentimental jewellery of the period, such as padlocks, hearts and serpents. The scarcity of emeralds during the 19th century is probably due to the fact that much of the output from the Colombian mines was snapped up by Eastern potentates; certainly, Victorian emerald jewellery is hardly abundant, although by the 20th century the gem enjoyed a visible revival. Poorer, flawed gems (more beryl than emerald) were popular in Arts and Crafts jewellery due to their gentle, subtle colours, whilst in the 1920s and 1930s fine quality stones were cut into rectangles and set in platinum as line bracelets, architectural pendants, double clip brooches and earrings contrasting with lines of baguette diamonds or the eternally popular three-stone ring.

PRECIOUS BLACK OPAL

Opal is a non-crystalline material composed of hardened silica gel and up to 20% water. Opals which exhibit several different colours of the

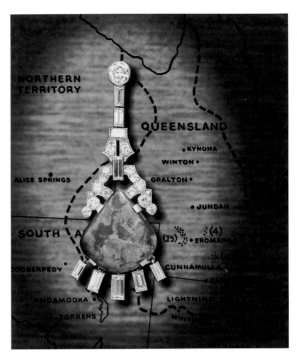

Art Deco 'Lightning Ridge' black opal and diamond pendant c.1930. The map indicates the location of Lightning Ridge in Queensland. Hancocks

rainbow within a deep grey, blue or black background are described as harlequin black opals and the unique 'play' of colour is known as the gem's 'pinfire'.

The majority of black opals are mined at Lightning Ridge, Queensland, Australia in conditions which are both arduous and exceedingly inhospitable, where subterranean labyrinthine tunnels have been carved out by hand. It is extremely unusual to find black opal jewellery before the end of the 19th century, although the material was used extensively in Arts and Crafts necklaces and pendants and Art Nouveau jewels where the highly individual and colourful gems were ideal for carving and shaping into naturalistic forms such as butterfly wings or imaginative figurative shapes such as sails.

Opal was popular in Edwardian and 'Belle Époque' platinum and diamond jewellery, usually taking the form of a simple oval plaque or domed cabochon in a border of brilliant-cut diamonds.

Chinese Imperial jade carved pendant suspended from a pink tourmaline and pearl ball c.1910.

Occasionally rubies, emeralds or green demantoid garnets were used as an effective contrast in colour. Black opals are exceptionally expensive today and it is unusual to find specimen gems in modern European manufactured jewellery. Opals which exhibit only blue and green pinfire are also, somewhat confusingly, known as black opals; however, these are usually correspondingly less valuable. Whatever the colour, care should be taken to ensure that any opal you may consider buying is free of chips, cracks and fractures.

IMPERIAL, OR PRECIOUS, JADEITE

Like black opal, jadeite was seldom used in European jewellery before the 20th century although Imperial jade, mined in Burma and carved in China, has been carved into amulets and pendants for 3,000 years. The colour of jade varies enormously, ranging from white to black, as well as yellow, brown and lavender, although the term 'Imperial jade' describes a rich emerald green tone, almost glass-like in its translucency and polish. Jade symbolises eternity and longevity and carvings frequently depict symbols associated with good luck such as bats, monkeys and dragons. Peaches and peonies

represent happiness, whilst pomegranates symbolise fertility and children.

To a great extent the West barely understands or appreciates the subtleties and potential value of jade which is why the major international auction houses hold their sales in the Far East where polished cabochons set into rings, carved earrings, hoop bangles and, especially, rows of graduated beads can easily fetch hundreds of thousands or even millions of dollars. Nevertheless, it is perfectly possible to purchase quite reasonable *non-precious* jade at auction or in the retail sector closer to home, although examples are unlikely to be particularly old and may exhibit irregularities in colour, clarity and quality.

ALEXANDRITE

Discovered in the Russian Urals in 1830, this singular gem was named in honour of Tsar Alexander II. A variety of chrysoberyl, it exhibits one fascinating property which makes it eminently desirable and correspondingly expensive – it changes colour depending upon the prevailing lighting conditions. The very finest 'old-mine' Russian stones alter from a deep bluish-green tone in natural light to raspberry-red in artificial and are usually found as small cushion-shaped stones in 19th century Russian pendants and brooches. Alexandrites of five carats or more are extremely rare although occasionally specimen gems do appear in fine diamond 'Belle Époque' settings. Ceylon alexandrites are less pronounced in colour change and recent finds in Brazil of excellent quality have been appearing on the market, although these stones do not have quite the desirability of their antique Russian counterparts. Synthetic corundum, which changes colour from purplish-blue to red, is prac-

Colour change in alexandrite: a bluish-green tone in natural light (left) and deep raspberry-red in artificial light (right).

tically worthless and has been sold as 'alexandrite' since the 1950s. Cheap stones described as 'alexandrite' should thus be treated with great caution and scepticism.

Mid-19th century 'Siberian' amethyst and gold portrait brooch. Russian amethysts exhibit a particularly desirable depth of 'Imperial' purple.

SEMI-PRECIOUS STONES

AMETHYST

A transparent variety of crystalline quartz, amethyst ranges in colour from very pale mauve to deep purple. Versatile and distinctive, amethyst was used by ancient Romans and Greeks for intaglio seal stones and was favoured by the Church for bishops' rings and pectoral crosses. The finest stones originated from Siberia although the majority of amethysts used in 19th century jewellery were from Brazil and Uruguay. Amethyst was particularly effective when mounted in yellow gold and was frequently accompanied by half pearls, diamonds and enamel. Scottish 'pebble' jewellery contained amethysts cut into the shape of thistles and late Victorian fringe necklaces were popular where the amethysts were set in graduated lines accompanied by compatible gems such as aquamarines and peridots. In the 1940s and 1950s amethyst was used in large scale gold brooches and bracelets cut into rectangles and mounted with unusual gem combinations such as turquoise and citrine.

AQUAMARINE

The pale transparent blue variety of beryl, aquamarine was the ideal accompaniment for elaborate early 19th century cannetille or floral work parures where the gem's subtle tone contrasted perfectly with fashionably delicate and feminine gold frames. The majority of these earlier aquamarine pieces were backed with foil to enhance their colour and brilliance and it was only in the 20th century that it was discovered that the blue colour could be intensified by heat treating. This resulted in large and bold rectangular aquamarines being mounted in Art Deco diamond and platinum architectural frames, a theme which extended through the 1950s when the gem often appeared in gold 'Retro' style settings.

(Left) Unusual amethyst cameo and diamond pendant c.1900. Woolley & Wallis

(Right) Belle Époque aquamarine and platinum diamond-set pendant c.1910. This aquamarine is especially appealing because of its excellent colour. Woolley & Wallis

Golden chrysoberyl and enamel Revivalist pendant c.1875. Woolley & Wallis

Although world distribution is widespread, the finest quality gems originate from Brazil where fairly massive crystals have been discovered. Aquamarine is frequently confused with blue topaz and synthetic blue spinel and it is recommended that pieces made after the 1950s are tested for authenticity.

CHRYSOBERYL

Chrysoberyl is a confusing gem since it comprises a family of three totally different stones of dis-associated appearance and value – Alexandrite (described in Precious Gems), Chrysoberyl and Chrysoberyl Cat's-eye.

Chrysoberyl

Although large pale yellowish green gems were used occasionally in mid-19th century gold pendants and brooches, smaller clusters of the stone were more commonly used in 18th and early 19th century English and Continental jewellery where it was known as *Chrysolite*. In Spain and Portugal, pavé-set clusters of chrysolites were fashioned as large navette-shaped dress rings or incredibly long bow and drop earrings whilst the gem enjoyed something of a revival in the 1870s, when it was set in colourful Neo-Renaissance enamel and cabochon garnet necklaces and pendants inspired by the paintings of Hans Holbein.

Chrysoberyl Cat's-eyes

Historically known as cymophane, chrysoberyl cat's-eyes are always polished *en cabochon* to exhibit their singular optical effect known as *chatoyancy* – a sharp band of light running from the top to the bottom of the centre of the stone. The finest stones are either honey green or olive green and originated in Ceylon and India. They were thought to ward off the evil eye and were thus highly prized. Chrysoberyl cat's-eyes should not be confused with quartz cat's-eyes which are coarser and far cheaper.

Chrysoberyl cat's-eye and diamond cluster ring c.1900.

CITRINE

A variety of crystalline quartz ranging in colour from the palest lemon through orange and brown, citrine has been used extensively in 19th and 20th century jewellery and ornamentation due to its abundance and modest value. The stone is often confused with *topaz*, but citrine lacks the brilliance of topaz and, when examined under a magnifying lens, often exhibits varying patches of colour. Citrine was widely used in gold and silver necklaces and bracelets and was so popular in Victorian Scottish jewellery that it was known as 'Cairngorm'. Early Victorian desk seals were sometimes made with faceted citrine handles which are desirable today; however, care should be taken to ensure that what is thought to be citrine is not actually paste. Like amethyst, citrine was popular in the 1940s and 1950s when large, rectangular stones in contrasting shades of yellow, gold and brown were set into architectural mounts.

Smoky Quartz

A common dark brown transparent quartz principally used in Scottish jewellery and cheaper late 19th century necklaces, brooches and bracelets where it was usually mounted in silver. Smoky quartz was

Scottish amethyst, citrine and silver thistle brooch c.1870. Scottish citrines are often described as 'cairngorms'. Brian and Lynn Holmes

Late 19th century Bohemian garnet jewellery. Vivid and effective, this variety of Middle European deep-red pyrope garnet was extremely common in the 1880s and 1890s. Examples are invariably mounted in low-grade gold or gilt metal.   RBR Group at Grays; Pat Novissimo

also fashionable for accessories such as desk seal handles, vinaigrettes and snuff boxes.

GARNET

Once upon a time garnet jewellery was abundant and modestly priced, but recent prices for good antique pieces have resulted in a rapid and justifiable reassessment of their status.

Garnet is found in several colours although red is by far the most common. There are two distinct red varieties found in antique jewellery:

Pyrope Garnet

Blood red garnet used extensively in the 18th and 19th century. Georgian pyrope garnets were invariably flat cut and oval in shape, set in gold and frequently foiled to improve their appearance. Common Georgian designs included cushion-shaped

brooches with half pearl decoration and hair locket centres, flower spray brooches, graduated collet rivières and necklaces of foliate design sometimes suspending below a Maltese cross pendant convertible to a brooch.

19th century pyrope garnets were used abundantly during the 'Grand' period of mid-Victorian opulence and were ideal gems for the extravagant effect. A popular fashion involved cutting garnets *en cabochon* and hollowing out the backs to 'lighten' the look of the stones. Cabochon garnets are often referred to as 'carbuncles'. Pyrope garnets were used in late 19th century Czechoslovakian and German jewellery in pavé-set clusters of multi-faceted stones. Known as Bohemian garnets, they were usually mounted in low grade gold or gilt metal in hundreds of different designs, from modest brooches to elaborate teardrop necklaces.

Garnet and pearl parure in its original fitted case c.1825.

Almandine Garnet

Claret or purplish-red garnet, more commonly used in 19th century 'carbuncle' jewellery such as French enamel and gold Neo-Renaissance 'Holbeinesque' pendants and necklaces where it was often accompanied by chrysolites.

The other principal varieties of garnet are:

Hessonite Garnet

A deep reddish-orange variety of grossular garnet. Hessonites were used in 19th century earrings, pendants and fringe necklaces in which they were fashionably known as 'jacinths'. They are distinctive for their unusual treacle-like inclusions.

Demantoid Garnet

By far the most valuable member of the garnet family, demantoids are a beautiful leaf-green variety of andradite garnet discovered in the Ural mountains and used predominantly in late 19th century figurative jewellery such as butterfly and lizard brooches, usually accompanied by diamonds, opals, half pearls or white enamel. Demantoids above 3 to 4 carats are rare and can fetch several thousand dollars per carat. They contain characteristic inclusions of hair-like asbestos known as 'horsetails.'

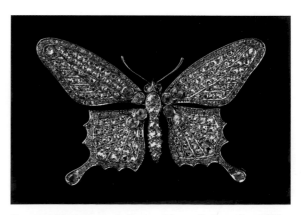

Demantoid garnet and diamond butterfly brooch c.1890.
Bentley & Skinner

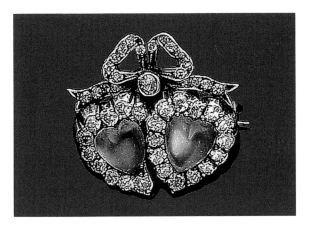

Turn of the century milky opal and diamond quatrefoil cluster ring.
Wimpole Antiques

Moonstone and diamond sentimental twin-heart brooch. This example is an excellent copy of a Victorian original.
Woolley & Wallis

MOONSTONE

A variety of feldspar, moonstone is appropriately named as it displays a bluish-white sheen effect known as adularescence. The stone is still extensively mined in Ceylon and India and was rarely used in jewellery before the end of the 19th century when the subtle, understated property of the stone was found to be ideal for naturalistic silver and gold brooches, pendants and necklaces. Moonstone is practically always polished *en cabochon* to exhibit its unique lustre. When cut into figurative designs, such as the head of an Egyptian Pharoah or a 'man in the moon', the value increases sharply, especially when enhanced by settings of diamonds.

OPAL
Milky opal

Milky opals were commonly used in late 19th century jewellery when their sheer versatility resulted in a wide assortment of designs such as bangles, set as a line of graduated cabochons with diamonds in between, cluster rings, fringe necklaces and crescent brooches. Superior examples exhibit an attractive play of red, green and blue colours whilst inferior milky opals are almost completely white with minimal flashes. Milky opals were also set with rubies, emeralds and demantoid garnets in naturalistic designs such as butterflies. Mid-Victorian opals exhibiting a softer play of colour were sometimes set in scrolling gold brooches and necklaces enamelled in royal blue.

Mexican fire opals

These vibrant gems were used in Art Nouveau and Art Deco diamond jewellery. Fire opal is usually deficient of any 'play' of colour but exhibits a singular shade of translucent mid- to deep orangy-red.

Opal doublets and triplets are fairly common in jewellery manufactured after the 1950s and were occasionally set in Arts and Crafts silver jewellery. The setting often concealed the fact that the opal was actually a 'sandwich' of two or three different materials and care should be taken to ensure that what appears to be a fine opal is not actually a composite.

PERIDOT

Formerly known as olivine, peridot is routinely confused with chrysolite, the yellowish green variety of chrysoberyl. The finest peridots are a deep lime-green colour and originated from the island of St John in the Red Sea. The stone has been set in jewellery since the time of the Romans although practically all the material on the market today is either Victorian or later. Peridots were sometimes used in 18th century fob seals and in the 1840s were mounted in elaborate gold scrolling settings and sold as parures complete with tiara, necklace, pair of bracelets and very long pendent earrings. The stone is particularly common in late 19th century open-work pendants, bar brooches and fringe necklaces invariably accompanied by half pearls in 9 or 15

Peridot and diamond necklace c.1905.

Bentley & Skinner

carat gold settings. Peridots can be identified by their characteristic 'doubling of the back facets' when viewed under a magnifying lens; modern examples are often rather pale and insipid.

ROCK CRYSTAL

The colourless variety of quartz used since earliest times as an ornamental stone in large scale objects of vertu such as vases, ewers and caskets and extensively in small scale jewellery and decorative accessories. Usually polished *en cabochon,* rock crystal formed the back covers of jewelled lockets or were engraved and painted from behind with naturalistic subjects

Victorian rock crystal pendant painted in reverse with a heron by the riverside c.1870.

such as insects, birds and domestic animals. These 'reverse crystals' were mounted in gold as pendants or brooches and are highly collectable today. Other Victorian rock crystal jewels included gold fringe necklaces in which rock crystal cabochons were decorated with diamond and ruby 'flies', necklaces mounted with pink foiled rock crystal imitating pink topaz and butterfly brooches where rock crystal plaques covered real butterfly wings.

Rock crystal was used widely in Belle Époque and Art Deco diamond jewellery, cut into architectural shapes and mounted with sapphires, rubies and – most effectively – coral and onyx. The stone was favoured by Fabergé in accessories such as bell pushes, vases of flowers and photograph frames and in the 1950s and 1960s, frosted rock crystal was popular in Austrian flower brooches in which the petals were sometimes stained in a variety of different colours.

SPINEL

Spinel is a gemstone which is surprisingly obscure in Western European jewellery but conversely was liberally used and highly valued in India where it was set into marvellous and flamboyant necklaces, bangles and earrings by the Mughal Emperors.

17th and 18th century Indian spinels are rare and costly and were usually cut into irregular pebble-like drops or were mounted in settings of gold as flat, table-cut stones accompanied by pearls, enamel and

(Left) Indian pink spinel and seed pearl earrings c.1800-1850.

(Right) Pink topaz, chrysolite, peridot and diamond cruciform pendant c.1830.
Bentley & Skinner

(Below) Imperial topaz and diamond brooch c.1915.
S.J. Phillips

mirror-back diamonds. The principal colour of spinel is a bright fiery-red which is often confused with ruby; the huge 'Black Prince's Ruby' mounted in the Imperial State Crown is actually a red spinel. Indeed, in earlier times spinels were routinely described as 'Balas rubies'. Spinels in 18th and early 19th century European settings are usually pinkish-red in colour and originated in Burma and Ceylon. Other colours used in antique jewellery include blue, purple and near-colourless.

Synthetic blue spinels appear deceptively like aquamarines but are usually a deeper blue tone. They were used in Continental jewellery after the 1950s and should be tested for authenticity.

TOPAZ

A beautiful transparent gemstone of which the three best known colours are golden brown, pink and blue. Precious or 'Imperial' topaz is a distinctive 'sherry' colour and was used in 18th century and later gold and diamond set jewellery in which the stone's

naturally bright and glittery appearance was often further enhanced by foiling. The finest topaz originated in Brazil and examples of good size and colour are extremely expensive today. Early 19th century sherry topaz was sometimes set in graduated rivières or in parures of necklace, bracelets and earrings in elaborate gold cannetille work settings. Pink topaz were set in a similar fashion, sometimes with cruciform-shaped gold pendants suspended below the necklace. Pink topaz was used sympathetically in early 19th century sentimental heart and padlock jewels where its pretty, pastel colour formed the perfect partnership with half pearls.

Topaz has a characteristic 'greasy' or slippery feel quite unlike stones of similar colour such as citrine or zircon. In the 19th century much citrine was erroneously called 'citrine topaz', especially in Scotland. Blue topaz has become a common and liberally used gemstone in modern gold and silver jewellery, although much of the material on the market today is heat treated.

TOURMALINE

A multi-coloured gemstone of which the two most popular shades are deep green and deep pink. As with several semi-precious gemstones, tourmaline gained widespread popularity at the end of the 19th century in gold pendants, necklaces and brooches of naturalistic design set with half pearls, aesthetic Arts and Crafts jewellery and subsequently in 1940s and 1950s gold brooches and bracelets. Pink tourmaline, more commonly known as *Rubellite*, was used in Chinese

Gold brooch c.1895 set with green tourmaline, half pearls and a pink tourmaline drop. This combination of colours is sometimes associated with the Suffragette movement.
John Joseph

Turquoise and pearl eagle brooch designed by Prince Albert for Queen Victoria's bridesmaids.   Wartski

carvings such as scent bottles and pendants suspended from jade balls. Care should be taken not to confuse the material with paler and more modestly priced rose quartz. 'Watermelon' tourmaline is an appropriately named variety exhibiting both green and pink colours, while *indicolite* is rarely seen blue tourmaline.

TURQUOISE

A prominent gemstone from the 18th century onwards, turquoise is well known for its opaque, waxy lustre and unique sky blue colour. The best examples originated in Persia and Egypt. During the 19th century, turquoise cut 'en cabochon' was used extensively in sentimental brooches, pendants, bracelets and rings due to its association with forget-me-nots; gold settings in several colours were often highly embellished and decorated with turquoise half pearls or rubies. Turquoise was widely used in early Victorian serpent jewellery although many of the stones seen today are badly discoloured and need replacing. Mid-Victorian turquoises were *pavé*-set in side-by-side formation and mounted into locket-back gold brooches and earrings with tassel fringes below. In the 1870s it became fashionable to mount oval gold lockets with turquoises cut into simple pyramids and set in geometric lines with rose diamonds or half pearls in between.

Of all gemstones, turquoise is probably the one which is most closely associated with the Arts and Crafts Movement. Designers including C.R. Ashbee

at the Guild of Handicraft and Archibald Knox for Liberty & Co produced many simple and uncomplicated gold and silver pendants and necklaces mounted with gem turquoise or turquoise matrix – turquoise with natural veins of limonite rock left visible. Indeed, the Anglo-German firm of Murrle Bennett & Co became synonymous with turquoise matrix and gold jewellery at the very end of the 19th century. Today, turquoise matrix is produced in large and irregular shape pebble-like forms used in Navajo Indian and New Mexican silver jewellery.

ZIRCON

Another 'aesthetic' late 19th century gemstone used by Revivalist jewellers such as Giuliano, zircon was mounted in commercial quantities after the 1920s in

Unusually large blue zircon and diamond architectural pendant c.1925.

Regency agate cushion-shaped plaque bracelet c.1800.

Art Deco diamond architectural settings and particularly finger rings. In Indian 19th century jewellery, colourless zircons, known as *jargoons,* were set in silver and mounted in turban ornaments or brooches. Most of the zircon on the market today has been heat treated and sometimes a treated stone will revert to its original colour, such as blue turning brown.

The majority of zircons are brownish-green, orange, blue or colourless. The availability of the stone after the Second World War led to many large three-dimensional brooches and bracelets being made with a combination of several different shades of orange and brown, whilst blue zircons from Ceylon were set into graduated lines in low grade white gold or silver.

Zircon exhibits a natural fire and brilliance which has frequently resulted in colourless zircon being sold as diamond. Examination under a 10x lens will reveal strong double refraction of the back facets and a feature practically unknown in a real diamond – abrasions and chips on the stone's surface.

ORNAMENTAL HARDSTONES

CHALCEDONY

Most of the hardstones familiar to us in jewellery – cameos, intaglios, Scottish pebbles, the bases of antique seals, to name but a few – are actually different coloured varieties of chalcedony. True chalcedony is greyish-white in colour and was used in Victorian brooches where the neutral tone of the material was sometimes offset by applying a spray of turquoise and gold forget-me-nots to the front. White chalcedony was also polished into teardrops and mounted in gold elongated pendent earrings and, strikingly, cut into triangular plaques and set into Maltese crosses with turquoise or ruby filigree gold decoration. The other principal varieties of chalcedony are:

Agate

This chalcedony is composed of strong, curved bands of colour and was invariably stained to display the contrasting shades. Used liberally in decorative carvings and jewellery, different names describe the various colours.

Bloodstone

Dark spinach green chalcedony with bright red spots of iron oxide. Formerly known as 'heliotrope', the red spots represented Christ's blood. Used in desk seals, Victorian fobs and gentlemen's signet rings.

Gold dog seal with oval bloodstone base. The red flecks were, in historic times, supposed to represent Christ's blood.
Michael Longmore

29

Green chrysoprase, ruby and diamond heart brooch c.1895. The subtle pastel tone of chrysoprase was popular in 1830s gold cannetille jewellery in which large oval shaped stones were set in delicate filigree frames. John Joseph

Typical cornelian seal stone on a Victorian embossed gold seal.
Wimpole Antiques

Banded onyx Etruscan style revival earrings c.1865.
Brian and Lynn Holmes

Chrysoprase

Apple green chalcedony of uniform colour, chrysoprase was used in 18th century jewellery in parures of gold or pinchbeck and in Arts and Crafts and Art Nouveau jewellery where the stone's charming understated colour was the perfect accompaniment for naturalistic gold settings.

Cornelian

Apparently uniform tawny-red or orangy-red but often banded when held up to the light, cornelian was extensively used in intaglio carving, fob seals and in Regency necklaces where polished cushion-shaped plaques were mounted in 'Roman' style seal settings.

Jasper

Mottled brown chalcedony used in Scottish pebble jewellery and often stained blue to suggest lapis lazuli, known as *Swiss Lapis*.

Moss Agate

Chalcedony with curiously realistic black or green fern-like structures. Used in 18th century necklaces, pairs of bracelets and snuff boxes.

Onyx

Black and white agate, ideal for cutting as cameos or polishing into beads. Used liberally in Victorian mourning jewellery where the jet-black hardstones exhibited a contrasting band of white at the edges.

Sardonyx

Brown and white agate principally used in Victorian cameos.

FLUORSPAR

The best known variety of fluorspar is Bluejohn, sometimes called Derbyshire Spar. This purple to light brown material is unique to the Castleton area of Derbyshire and was mainly used in ornamental carvings such as vases and bowls as well as small-scale jewellery.

LABRADORITE

A greyish blue feldspar exhibiting rainbow-like flashes of colour and used in the 19th century for cutting into ornaments and cameos.

LAPIS LAZULI

An intense blue material containing flecks of golden colour iron pyrites, lapis lazuli has been used as an ornamental hardstone since ancient times. Lapis can vary widely in quality; the best material is a uniform royal blue colour mined in Afghanistan and Russia,

Gold hoop architectural earrings with lapis lazuli sphere finials c.1870.

whilst inferior Chilean and American lapis usually contains veins of white calcite. Lapis lazuli was used in Victorian gold jewellery in the form of beads, polished cabochons or sometimes conical-shaped drops in fringe necklaces. Early lapis was sometimes cut into cameos and Egyptian and Roman lapis intaglios were popular as seal stones.

In Art Deco jewellery, lapis lazuli was cut into geometric shapes and used in brooches, bracelets and mantel clocks favoured by the firm of Cartier and its contemporaries.

MALACHITE

A distinctive, marbled or banded green hardstone which was used in decorative ornaments such as candlesticks, desk accessories and table tops. The finest malachite originated in Russia; other deposits are found in Zaire and South Africa. Malachite jewellery includes early 19th century cameos carved with classical heads or groups and Scottish silver jewellery where malachite panels were cut into circular plaid brooches, ivy leaf necklaces and broad panel link bracelets. Modern malachite is usually fashioned into animal carvings or necklaces of graduated beads.

NEPHRITE JADE

The ornamental dark spinach-green variety of jade, nephrite was favoured by Fabergé for objects of vertu including bell pushes and cigarette cases as well as small accessories such as cufflinks. This

Victorian malachite and gold desk seal in its original fitted case c.1840.

Gold cigarette case with nephrite jade covers. 'Spinach' green jade is darker and less valuable than precious jadeite. It was used extensively in accessories and functional objets d'art such as cufflinks, seals and desk sets. Michael Longmore

Arts and Crafts silver pendant mounted with a rose quartz cabochon in a frame of pink-foiled moonstones and mother-of-pearl. The soft, understated pastel tones of rose quartz make it an ideal gem for this kind of aesthetic jewel.
RBR Group at Grays

material was extracted in Siberia although most of the nephrite jade seen today originates from New Zealand. Nephrite is usually cut into simple and fairly inexpensive souvenir jewellery – heart pendants and brooches bearing 'national symbols' such as fern leaves in gold, amuletic pendants called 'tikis' and bead necklaces on simple clasps.

ROSE QUARTZ

A pale pink variety of cloudy crystalline quartz used in objects of vertu and jewellery particularly from the late 19th century onwards. Common themes include animal carvings, necklaces of graduated beads and silver jewellery mounted with large rose quartz cabochons.

ORGANIC MATERIALS

PEARL

Arguably the most important gem material next to the diamond, pearls are surprisingly robust con-

sidering they are an entirely natural organic material. Pearls are found in many different shapes and colours and were usually worn to designate status, authority and power. In the 16th century, natural pearls from the Persian Gulf were drilled and strung as elaborate ropes or mounted on to halo-like *biliments* to be worn in the hair. At the same time, curiously-shaped baroque pearls suggesting grotesque animal, bird or mythical forms were mounted in gold and worn as pendants. Pearls were even crushed and swallowed for their assumed medicinal and restorative properties curing maladies as diverse as stomach ulcers and cholera.

Pearls are an accident of nature, formed in living molluscs such as oysters and mussels. When a foreign object such as a grain of sand or grit finds its way into the shell, the mollusc secretes layer upon layer of a smooth material called *conchiolin* around the irritant which gradually builds up over time into a pearl.

There are five important factors which influence the rarity and value of pearls:

Two-row natural pearl necklace on emerald and diamond snap c.1920.
Woolley & Wallis

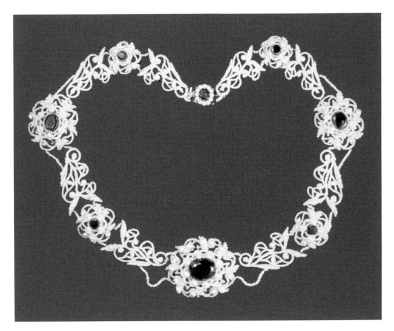

Seed pearl and garnet woven necklace c.1845.

Natural pearl and diamond brooch with matching drop c.1895.

Size. Whether natural or cultured, the larger the pearl the greater its value.

Shape. A perfectly round pearl will command a higher price than another which is off-round or baroque in shape.

Colour. There are a bewildering number of different colours available in 'modern' cultured pearls, although natural pearls in antique jewellery are invariably white, grey to gunmetal, bronze, cream or yellow. Pearls with unsightly spots of brown will be correspondingly less valuable

Purity. Since pearls are a natural organic material, they are prone to irregularities, spots, blemishes and damage. Pearls will often wear down around the drill holes in necklaces whilst cultured pearls invariably exhibit 'blisters', 'holes' and surface imperfections.

Lustre. The beautiful iridescent surface of a pearl is described as its nacre. The thicker the nacre, the higher the lustre and the greater the value. Cultured pearls are often farmed early in the pearl's development resulting in thin, lifeless nacre which sometimes peels away to reveal the artificial bead nucleus underneath.

Natural Pearls

Before the introduction of cultured pearls at the beginning of the last century, natural or *Oriental* pearls were extremely costly. In the 1920s a fairly modest necklace of graduated pearls could easily sell for several hundred pounds. Natural pearls were imported into Europe from the Arabian Gulf, Japan, the Gulf of Manaar off North West Ceylon, Australia, California and Venezuela. There are numerous different names of natural pearls dependent upon individual shape, size and colour.

(i) *Baroque pearls.* The name given to irregular-shaped pearls common in 16th and 17th century Continental jewellery and subsequently in 19th century Revivalist pendants and brooches. Baroque pearls were often large and imperfect, although pairs mounted in earrings are always in high demand.

(ii) *Blister pearls.* Extremely distorted baroque pearls used in naturalistic Arts and Crafts and Art Nouveau jewellery. Narrow, elongated drops were known as Mississippi pearls.

(iii) *Bouton pearls.* Pearls with rounded tops and flat bases used in 19th and 20th century decorative

33

Pink conch pearl, black and white natural pearl and diamond 'Ace of Clubs' c.1885.

diamond and gem-set jewellery.

(iv) *Seed pearls*. Very small pearls used in Victorian jewellery where the individual pearls were woven on to mother-of-pearl backplates in decorative floral clusters. Edwardian sautoirs consisted of several strands of seed pearls woven into ropes with tassel finials. Woven seed pearl jewellery is prone to deterioration and damage which reduces its value significantly.

(v) *Freshwater pearls*. Sometimes called Mussel pearls, freshwater pearls are found in rivers and inland waters. Predominantly white, freshwater pearls tend towards a dull lustre. Scottish freshwater pearls were used from the Middle Ages.

(vi) *Mother-of-pearl*. The iridescent shell of the mollusc which was cut and shaped into 'backing plates' for seed pearl clusters and Victorian lockets and portrait brooches. In the 1920s mother-of-pearl was popular in gentlemen's accessories such as cufflinks.

(vii) *Pink Pearls*. This category of natural pearl is extracted from a mollusc called the Great Conch. Pink pearls exhibit characteristic flame-like markings on their surface. Often confused with coral, pink pearls were popular in Belle Époque diamond jewellery whilst drop-shaped specimens were mounted as tiepins. Pink pearls are rare and can achieve high prices at auction, although irregular discoloured patches will reduce their value.

Cultured pearls

Pearls created artificially by inserting a small bead of glass or mother-of-pearl into the mollusc and farming the resulting product on a commercial scale. The introduction of cultured pearls in the 1920s all but destroyed the market for natural pearls. Necklaces of cultured pearls up to 9mm (⅜in.) in diameter were extremely fashionable up to the 1960s, but their appeal has declined quite markedly so today it is only the 'new' cultured pearls from the South Seas and Australia which are commercially exploited. These pearls are farmed in sizes of 20mm (¾in.) or more and occur in many different colours, shapes and quality.

Mabé pearls. Cultured pearls often of quite large size composed of a 'skin' of cultured pearl over a bead nucleus with mother-of-pearl 'jacket.' Used in contemporary Continental jewellery and mounted into rings and earclips.

Artificial Pearls

An important category of imitation gem, artificial pearls have been used in jewellery set with diamonds and costume jewellery since the Renaissance. Early imitation pearls consisted of hollow opalescent glass beads which were sprayed with *essence d'orient*, a

Faux pearl and rose diamond earrings c.1795. Composed of glass hollow beads coated with varnish and ground fish-scales, such false pearls are fragile and rarely found today.

solution composed primarily of fish scales. These 'pearls' were fragile and had the same composition as Christmas tree baubles. It is likely that many of the so-called pearl necklaces in early paintings were actually imitation. Most modern artificial pearls are simply sprayed glass beads.

Coq de perle. Large sections of mother-of-pearl and nautilus shell backed with cement and often set in frames of marcasite. Coq de perle or 'eggshell pearls' were fashionable in early 19th century necklaces and earrings.

AMBER

Amber is fossilised resin which oozed from certain types of coniferous trees flourishing millions of years ago. Occasionally, the sticky sap would trap a tiny insect or leaf particle in its slow descent so producing the rare material much sought and frequently faked today.

Probably the best known variety of amber used in antique jewellery is *Baltic* found near Konigsberg, East Prussia and on the Lithuanian coastline. Typically cloudy yellow or opaque honey yellow, Baltic amber is polished into graduated beads, cut into naturalistic brooches or fulfilled many practical uses including the handles of cutlery, the stems of pipes or the shafts of parasols. Scandinavian silversmiths such as Georg Jensen found the understated colours of Baltic amber to be ideal in silver jewellery and much of the amber sold today is heavily influenced by earlier Arts and Crafts naturalistic forms. Other varieties of amber include:

Chinese – usually imported from Burma, colours range from pale yellow to rich red. Examples include bead necklaces cut into complicated patterns and scent bottles of 18th century origin with jade stoppers.

Sicilian – deep brown or reddish with a distinctive bluish fluorescence.

Rumanian – often imperfect or cracked, this amber is deep brown or even black in colour.

Amber-like materials in common use since the end of the 19th century include:

A cloudy Baltic yellow amber necklace and a row of transparent golden brown amber beads. The red bead necklace at the top is copal resin, a dense and rather heavy material which is routinely mistaken for genuine amber.

Sylvie Spectrum

Pressed Amber (amboid) – small particles of Baltic amber softened by heating and pressed together into workable sections.

Copal Resin – routinely confused with amber, New Zealand copal resin is opaque russet brown and can be distinguished by applying a drop of ether which leaves a dull mark on the surface – no mark would be left on genuine amber.

Plastic, Bakelite and *Celluloid* – deceptively amberlike in appearance but will peel under a sharp knife unlike amber which splinters.

CORAL

Of all organic gem materials, coral was probably the most versatile in its use in antique gold jewellery. Coral is formed from the skeletons of millions of tiny marine animals called polyps and it is rather depressing to consider just how much of this wonderful – and irreplaceable – natural phenomenon

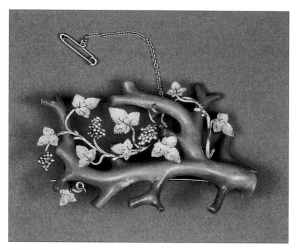

Italian branch coral and gold ivy leaf brooch signifying friendship and fidelity c.1850.

has been extracted from the deep seas in the past few hundreds of years.

Each distinct colour of coral bears its own name. Some of these include white (Bianco), Pelle d'Angelo (Angel's skin – an off-white with pinkish overtones), Rosa Vivo (bright rose), Russo (red) and black. The very deep red coral graphically known as Ox Blood is possibly the most expensive today with a top grade bead necklace selling for over $10,000 in specialist shops.

Coral never really lost popularity throughout the 19th century although designs certainly changed

significantly. During the late 18th and early 19th century gilt metal diadems were mounted with coral beads sometimes covered in small facets or even etched with finely-milled criss-crossing lines. In this essentially romantic period, floral spray brooches with white coral flowerheads were enhanced by turquoise and ruby stamens, early Victorian coral was cut into the shape of hands, cherubs and naturalistic sprays whilst by the 1850s and 1860s Italian workers based in Naples were transforming the branch-like shapes of the natural material into all sorts of imaginative designs such as sea monsters, grotesques and skulls – the latter especially fashionable in gentlemen's cravat pins. Salmon pink and pale pink coral was an ideal medium for carving into Classical cameos and during the height of Classical revivalism coral was polished into elongated tear-shaped drops and set into graduated fringe necklaces in bright yellow gold mounts. Since the colour of coral could be entirely neutral, it was ideal for either understated and modest dress rings or far more extravagant parures of several components with sky-blue enamel and diamond highlights.

During the 20th century coral was mounted in contrast with striking hardstones such as onyx, rock crystal and chalcedony. Since coral could be cut into flat plaques, pyramids or tubular batons, it was perfect for Art Deco 'architectural' brooches and bracelets favoured by Cartier in France and Theodor Fahrner in Germany. After the Second World War Italian goldsmiths such as Bulgari have successfully adapted coral into large and visual gold and diamond-set jewels of highly individual style.

IVORY

A material which was used in 17th and 18th century decorative objects and everyday accessories such as patch boxes, fans and bodkin cases. Before the 19th century ivory was somewhat limited in its use in jewellery to the backgrounds of miniatures or pretty carvings inside Regency locket rings and brooches. After the 1850s the obsession with naturalism resulted in ivory being cut and fashioned into brooches designed as floral bouquets, sprays of lily of the valley and autumnal wheatsheaves. Popular

Gold earrings set with foiled rock crystal cabochons within borders of white coral beads. White coral was a popular material in early Victorian gold flower spray brooches. John Joseph

A Victorian ivory cameo pendant and a carved ivory cherub brooch. Ivory is often confused with cheaper and far cruder bone which was used at the turn of the 19th/20th centuries in souvenir beads, brooches and rosaries.   Miss G. Benjamin; Sylvie Spectrum

from 1850 to 1880, these lifelike and imaginative carvings were somewhat let down by cheap silver or very basic gold pin fasteners at the back.

Ivory was also cut into bold cameos depicting classical female heads in profile; a Bacchante complete with bunches of grapes in her hair was particularly favoured. In German 19th century brooches ivory was cut with considerable skill and finesse into the design of woodland and rustic landscapes or hunting groups of horses, stags and hounds.

Care should be taken to ensure that what is considered to be ivory is not actually bone. The two materials are routinely confused; genuine ivory exhibits characteristic wavy lines whilst bone is coarser, lighter in weight and contains tiny black imperfections.

In Art Nouveau jewellery ivory was cut into stylised female or animal forms accompanied by plique-à-jour enamel decoration, whilst in Art Deco jewellery ivory was fashioned into geometric shapes and mounted in both silver and gold.

JET

In an age when black was the outstanding colour for some forty years, jet was synonymous with a Britain plunged into mourning after the death of Prince Albert in 1861.

Real jet is a kind of fossilised wood formed under intense heat and pressure. By far the most important location of the Victorian jet industry was Whitby situated on the coast of North Yorkshire, appropriately enough the setting for Bram Stoker's *Dracula*. Whitby jet takes a high polish and is surprisingly light in weight. It was carved into any number of ornaments and objects of art although it is most closely associated with mourning jewellery. Examples range from modest crosses, oval lockets and locket back brooches to far more elaborate bracelets and necklaces with drops and festoons. Jet and its use in the context of mourning jewellery is discussed in greater detail in the chapter entitled 'The Industry of Death.'

Materials similar in appearance to jet include:
Bog-oak – dull, dark brown wood from Irish peat bogs. Popular in the 1850s, bog-oak jewellery was often well cut into flowers or brooches of national flavour such as shamrocks.

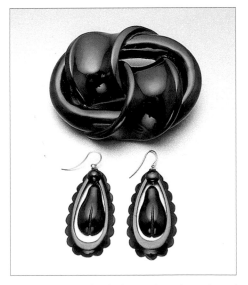

Victorian carved Whitby jet knot brooch and earrings c.1875.   Satoe; Sylvie Spectrum

French jet flower earrings c.1880. French jet is simply polished black glass and is both colder and heavier than jet.

Jet-like materials: a Victorian vulcanite cross and an Irish bog oak 'hand with fan' brooch.

Sylvie Spectrum; Pat Novissimo

Victorian tortoiseshell group c.1860 incorporating silver and gold floral inlay. The buckle is decorated with characteristic geometric patterns. Brian and Lynn Holmes

French jet – black glass. Much heavier than jet with a shiny patina and cold to the touch, French jet was used in 18th century brooches and hair locket rings and widely in late 19th century costume jewellery.

Vulcanite – *a*lso known as *gutta-percha*, vulcanite was a type of treated India rubber containing sulphur.

Other materials confused with jet include plastic, black onyx and black enamel.

SHELL
See Chapter 7: Cameos

TORTOISESHELL
It is unlikely that the Victorians gave much thought to issues such as endangered species. Certainly, if the staggering number of beetles, butterflies, humming-birds, turtles and tigers which were routinely exterminated in the name of Decorative Arts is anything to go by, we can only presume that they must have been supremely indifferent to the conservation of wildlife.

Tortoiseshell comes from the overlapping body plates of certain species of turtle, of which the principal contributor was the hawksbill turtle. Those plates taken from the back are dark mottled brown or reddish brown, whilst those from the underbelly are a uniform honey-brown colour, better known as blond tortoiseshell. The latter variety was used in haircomb fittings and in Art Deco vanity cases known as minaudières.

The manufacture of ivory and tortoiseshell into decorative objects and accessories can be traced

Rare and impressive Georgian rivière composed of precious and semi-precious gemstones and exhibiting a complete spectrum of colours.
S.J. Phillips

back to the 17th century when French Huguenot craftsmen produced elegant and highly practical snuff boxes, patch boxes, needlework cases and étui, inlaid with precious metals and decorated with chinoiserie designs and pretty patterns. Tortoiseshell becomes soft when heated, enabling the craftsman to bend and mould the material into the shape of the desired object. The surface was then polished and inlaid with mother-of-pearl, silver or gold in a technique known as 'pricking'. This gave rise to the word *piqué* and thus tortoiseshell piqué work.

Patterns of tiny stars, polka dots and bead clusters were known as 'piqué point' whilst strips of wire in floral cluster or geometric patterns were called 'piqué posé'. Both techniques were used in Victorian jewellery which originated in the 1830s and reached a peak of popularity by the 1860s. Brooches were particularly common. Fashioned as circular domed plaques or geometric in shape, they displayed bouquets of flowers or overlapping fish-scale designs. The backs of the brooches were hollowed out and the frames were mounted with simple metal or silver pins. Earrings sometimes take the form of elongated tear-drops known as pipkins. Other frequently seen designs include Maltese crosses, scalloped haircombs, buttons and large belt buckles. Necklaces and finger rings are rare.

Much of the piqué seen today is damaged with the gold and silver inlay deficient or the tortoiseshell cracked and faded. A fine quality brooch or pair of earrings will therefore sell at a considerable premium.

Further reading

Gems, Robert Webster (NAG Press)
Practical Gemmology, Robert Webster (NAG Press)
Gem Testing, Basil Anderson (Newnes-Butterworths)
The Dealer's Book of Gems & Diamonds, M. Sevdermish and A. Mashiah (KAL Painting House)

CHAPTER 2

THE EVOLUTION OF JEWELLERY FROM EARLY TIMES TO THE 18TH CENTURY

I believe there has never been a better time to collect old jewellery. True, the value of what might be described as 'primary' jewellery continues to climb as availability recedes and demand expands, but it is still perfectly possible to invest in pretty Victorian brooches, rings and bracelets at fairly modest prices, whilst numerous antique jewels and accessories such as seals, buckles, tiepins and dress studs can be purchased surprisingly cheaply simply because they are considered difficult to wear and, therefore, unfashionable. The trick is to identify which disciplines are undervalued and thus collectable before prices inevitably start to rise.

The wonderful thing about antique jewellery is that you will seldom find two pieces which match identically and so you have the added confidence of knowing that you are wearing a brooch, bracelet or buckle which nobody else will be able to imitate. A splendid $100,000 pearl necklace purchased from a leading international retailer certainly looks stunning but it can be replicated in any number of stores in a dozen different countries. An early Victorian gold cannetille work brooch set with aquamarines or pink topaz implies singular good taste, distinctive character and reinforces the suggestion that the person wearing it is breathtakingly chic. And all for less than £5,000.

Ancient Gold

Surprisingly enough, it is perfectly possible to buy at auction a simple Roman gold ring or pair of ancient earrings for under £2,000. Roman, Greek and Hellenistic seal stones were produced in very large quantities and were set into bright yellow gold or silver mounts of simple construction; earrings depicting heads of goddesses or with basic amphora (urn-shaped) drops are extremely pretty and appear in specialist auctions in London. Condition is paramount since many ancient gold artefacts were hollow and extremely soft and thus were liable to damage or crushing. The significant factor with ancient jewellery is that few people actually understand it and most dealers steer well clear of it, concentrating on more commercially mainstream periods. Unfortunately, the market is awash with fakes so it is important to buy from reliable sources where provenance is impeccable.

 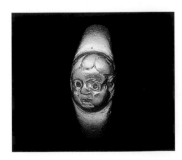

(Far left) Georgian gold ring mounted with a Roman hardstone cameo of an infant c.2nd-4th century AD. The popularity of neo-classicism at the end of the 18th century prompted widespread setting of ancient hardstones in contemporary mounts.

(Left) Roman gold ring, the bezel fashioned as an infant, 2nd century AD.

Gold ring brooch bearing an inscription, 13th-14th century.   S.J. Phillips

Saxon, Viking and Medieval Gold

The vast majority of gold rings, clasps, brooches and assorted jewels from the Dark Ages through the Viking occupation and well into the Middle Ages are invariably found by enthusiasts using metal detectors who scour the countryside, farmers' fields and the shoreline for these rare and precious artefacts. Finds such as these must, by law, be reported to the District Coroner who then decides whether the object should be declared Treasure Trove and either sold to an appropriate museum or returned to the finder.

Jewellery from this period can be extremely valuable, particularly if embellished with gems and enamel or decorated with a complicated device signifying that it originally belonged to a person of high rank. Nevertheless, more modest Saxon, Viking and later gold rings do find their way into the auction rooms and can be purchased at realistic price levels. Viking rings are especially beautiful and sophisticated, composed of entwined pale yellow

A group of four rings including three gold signets with engraved bezels, 15th and 16th centuries. Prosperous citizens and merchants in England and Germany wore heraldic gold rings for identification of legal documents as well as status in society.

gold wires wrought together into a tapering plait. Rings of the 12th and 13th centuries are usually simple and rather austere; the bezel or top of the ring is set with an irregular shaped polished gem – usually sapphire, ruby or garnet – which is cut en cabochon into a simple dome. 14th century religious gold rings known as iconographic rings are carefully engraved to depict the figures of saints, whilst 15th and early 16th century gold signet rings usually displayed the arms of a distinguished family in a simple shield device with accompanying inscription.

The 16th Century

Very little 'everyday' 16th century jewellery survives today. Most pieces are displayed in museums whilst those rings or pendants offered at

Medieval gold ring mounted with a simple sapphire bead cabochon c.1150-1250.

 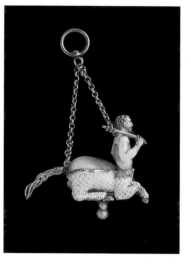 

16th century German enamelled gold and gem-set parrot pendant c.1580.
National Trust Waddesdon Manor

16th century Spanish baroque pearl, white enamel and gold centaur pendant. Note the way that the jewel has been imaginatively constructed to follow the contours of the pearls.
National Trust Waddesdon Manor

16th century German enamelled gold cross depicting symbols of the crucifixion and the armorials of Von Kienburg c.1580.   S.J. Phillips

auction tend to be either exceedingly expensive or so badly damaged as to render them unusable. Renaissance pendants were confined to a market made up of nobility or prosperous merchants and were fashioned from near pure gold decorated with polychrome enamel and studded with costly gems, particularly rubies, simple table-cut diamonds and (invariably) baroque-shaped pearls, known in the 16th century as *margarettes*. Religious and magical themes were important; devotional jewellery included rosaries (formerly called 'paternosters') and crosses set with emeralds and diamonds, much beloved of Spanish aristocracy. Cameos were surprisingly well carved in the 16th century depicting prominent individuals with unromanticised profiles or classical groups of figures fashioned from black and white onyx or chalcedony. Merchants' rings do occasionally appear at auction; massive and intentionally impressive, these chunky gold or silver signet rings were often engraved with a coat of arms directly on to the bezel or incised upon a transparent rock crystal plaque which was foiled in gold from behind and sometimes painted with a date signifying

the year in which it was constructed. Rings during this period were often carved with baroque scrolls and brightly coloured with enamel to offset fairly simple and unsophisticated gems. By the start of the 17th century much of this ornate embellishment had given way to a far more simplified style typical of Jacobean taste.

The 17th Century

In 1912 workmen digging in the sticky clay beneath the cellar of a shop in Friday Street in the City of London stumbled upon a decayed casket containing a large quantity of gold necklaces, rings, earrings, gemstones and assorted objets d'art. How such a comprehensive range of jewels came to be buried around the corner from St Paul's is a mystery – possibly it was the stock of a jeweller fleeing the Great Fire or even the ravages of the Plague. What is certain, however, is that the Cheapside Hoard, as the treasure came to be known, offers jewellery historians an unparalleled opportunity of viewing at first hand how 17th century jewellery was designed, constructed and decorated.

Casket of jewels, principally German 1600-1650, by Pieter Gerritsz. van Roestraten (c.1630-1700). Note the simple table-cut diamonds and rubies, the limit of technical achievement at the time.   Rafael Valls Gallery/Bridgeman Art Library

Apart from one or two 'grand' pieces such as a solid emerald crystal converted into a watch, the vast majority of items are clearly made for customers without limitless resources. Much of the jewellery is elegant, brightly coloured with enamel and set with table-cut gemstones. Chains are composed of enamelled floriate links while a pair of amethyst earrings are carved into the design of a bunch of grapes, appearing more Victorian than Jacobean in their inspiration. The Cheapside Hoard is on permanent

Pretty gold 'Ram' amulet jewel threaded with pearls and containing a hinged compartment at the base for a religious relic. Spanish Colonial or South Italian, c.1600-1620.

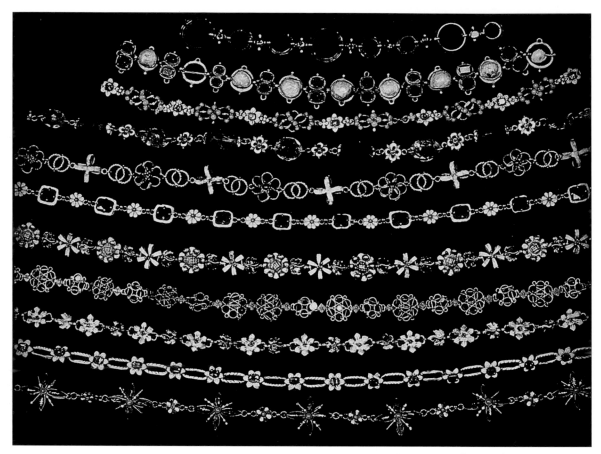

(Above) A group of early 17th century enamelled gold and gem-set necklaces from the London Cheapside Hoard.
Museum of London

(Below) Cheapside Hoard enamel, gold and gem-set rings exhibiting the elegance and colourful designs of 17th century English jewellery.
Museum of London

display at the Museum of London in the Barbican.

In the 17th century the dominant design in jewellery was the flower. Advances in diamond cutting resulted in the appearance of the *rose cut* and the flower in all its different forms was the ideal vehicle for showing off clusters of these little diamonds reflecting light from a series of triangular-shaped facets on the crown of each individual stone. Although gold settings were in use, the majority of gem-set jewellery was mounted in silver which extended to enclose fully the back of the jewel itself.

Enamel played an important part in the embellishment of much 17th century jewellery providing an effective substitute for expensive gems and effectively filling the spaces both on the front and

44

(Above) Gold slide painted with a miniature under crystal of Charles II c.1685. Memento Mori *jewels usually contained a fragment of the deceased's hair.*   S.J. Phillips

(Above right) Memento Mori *slide of James II c.1701.*
                                                          S.J. Phillips

back of an object. Specific colours were favoured, especially sky blue with white and black scrolling highlights (popular on the backs of lockets and miniatures), whilst English and Dutch necklaces and pendants often depicted charming and intricate sprays of roses and tulips in white and shades of pink. Many Stuart and later *Memento Mori* jewels were enamelled in this way, the exquisite little flowers providing a poignant counterbalance to the grim skeletons, coffins and woven hair embedded within.

From around 1620 to the middle part of the century, aristocratic ladies began to wear large and impressive jewels on the bodices of their gowns. Mounted in silver or silver gilt and set with a profusion of table-cut diamonds and coloured gems such as topaz, emerald or ruby, these splendid ornaments were further adorned with baroque-shaped pearl drops. The principal feature of these incredibly imposing creations was the bow, constructed as a series of elaborate looping ribbons gathered at the centre. It was the famous French writer of letters, Madame de Sévigné, who gave her name to this particular style of jewel – the *Sévigné* bow brooch.

Flamboyant brooches worn in the hair were known as *aigrettes*. Naturalistic in inspiration, aigrettes usually took the form of a spray of flowers or a feather-like plume. Set with diamonds or lines of coloured gems, they were the perfect vehicle for showing gems off at their best, especially when displayed beneath the twinkling light of chandeliers. It is interesting to note that James I, the so-called 'wisest fool in Christendom', sold off many of the best pieces from the Royal Collection to pay for one massive aigrette brooch known as 'The Feather', which he wore customarily in his hat.

Earrings followed this opulent trend with the gradual introduction of the *girandole* in which three pear-shaped drops were suspended from a principal top stone, often with a bow or flower-shaped cluster of smaller stones in between. The fashion for wearing girandole earrings and brooches of girandole form was to continue right up to the 19th century to be gradually superseded by less flamboyant and more practical styles in the 1840s and 1850s.

17th century Spanish jewellery was overwhelmingly devotional in design. Bright yellow gold crosses, pendants containing boxwood scenes from the Crucifixion and religious ornaments containing 'pieces of the True Cross' were studded with flat table-cut diamonds and the one coloured gem which took precedence over all others – the emerald. Carried along

 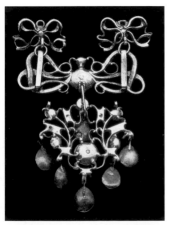

(Far left) Early 18th century silver, ruby and table-cut diamond baroque bow ornament, probably Spanish c.1720-1740. The gems are almost crude in their simplicity.

(Left) The same jewel in reverse exhibiting the flat, fully enclosed silver mount with elements of gilding still remaining. This ornament would have been worn on a velvet ribbon or suspended from a simple chain from the upper bows.

A fine Spanish 18th century emerald and gold bow and cruciform pendant brooch. S.J. Phillips

with fine and rare two hundred year old diamonds of a singular soft white purity.

The beauty and rarity of much 18th century jewellery reflects the growing importance of diamonds brought about by significant advances in the technique of cutting and polishing. For the first time the unrivalled sparkle of diamonds could be properly appreciated, especially when set in lines and clusters within many of the floral and naturalistic studies characteristic of the period.

By around 1720 the use of coloured enamel as the dominant feature of the complete jewel had all but disappeared and, although still a characteristic of Parisian jewellery, its application was largely confined to decoration on pretty accessories such as pomanders, étuis and chatelaines. The general trend was for settings (usually silver) to be left plain and unembellished. The influence of French ornamentation became increasingly important in jewellery and the decorative arts with the appearance of the new style of classical adornment known as *Rococo*. The so-called *Rocaille* fashion was observed in necklaces composed of scrolling sections, complicated floral embellishment and a strong lack of symmetry. By around 1750 brooches in the design of large and vibrant bouquets of flowers worn on the bodice became extremely popular, not just in England but throughout Europe. These splendid jewels could easily achieve lengths of well over eight inches (20cm) and were studded throughout with lovely 'old-mine' gemstones such as rubies, emeralds and sapphires in floral clusters faithfully replicating the genuine article. The enthusiasm for flowers in the

the dangerous trade routes between Europe and South America, emeralds are today strongly identified with Spanish and Portuguese jewellery although, sadly, many of these beautiful pieces are now totally unwearable and are frequently damaged.

The 18th Century

Whenever Georgian diamond jewellery comes up for auction you can be sure that competition will be fierce and prices will invariably rocket. Why should this be the case? The answer might be to take two diamond flower brooches, one made in 1775, the other in 1895. Whereas the late Victorian example will betray a rigid, machined construction with diamonds of variable colour and clarity and an altogether mass-produced finish, the Georgian flower by contrast will be fully enclosed in an elegant silver mount, the broad, uniform sized petals will display a powerful impression of lush naturalism and, above all, the brooch will be 'pavé-set' in side-by-side formation

Mid-18th century ruby and diamond bow and cluster necklace. English or French c.1750.

(Left) Splendid multi gem-set floral corsage brooch, probably English c.1720-1750. Such jewels were invariably mounted in silver and are extremely rare today. S.J. Phillips

(Right) Pavé diamond set oval cluster ring c.1800. Such Georgian diamonds often originated from dried-out river beds and exhibit a singular purity of colour and clarity. Woolley & Wallis

middle part of the 18th century was ideally illustrated in rings and brooches known as *Giardinetti* or 'Little Garden' jewels. These pretty floral studies combined diamonds set in silver cut-down collets with several vari-colour gems or pastes correspondingly set in gold. Sometimes, the principal gem – possibly a ruby or an emerald – would conform to the shape of a stylised vase or flower pot.

18th century rings are, almost without exception, elegant and very saleable today – which is why there are so many modern copies on the market, some of which are of high quality and many downright crude. Georgian rings were worn every day and often on every finger of the hand. This meant that they easily wore out so a genuine example in top condition will fetch a considerable premium over a similar ring with tell-tale rubbed shank and scratched or damaged setting.

The classic Georgian ring was set with a cushion-shaped flat-cut diamond or precious stone in a dome-back bezel (the top of the ring) within a border of small diamonds. This bezel was made of polished silver or gold which during the 1750s might be engraved with a series of radiating fluted lines known as 'sunburst' effect. Since the bezel was fully enclosed, light could not pass through the stone and therefore it became routine to place a piece of appropriately coloured tinfoil behind the gem to strengthen its colour and improve its 'sparkle'. This did create its own set of problems. Any water which leaked into the setting would discolour the foil (diamond foil, for example, turned a nasty charcoal grey) and, if the colour of a gemstone could be

'improved' by foiling, it was a natural progression to fake, say, a sapphire by placing a piece of blue tinfoil behind a worthless rock crystal or colourless paste. Very much a case of *caveat emptor,* I am sorry to say.

Opulent diamond bouquets and jewel encrusted brooches were all very well for those members of the aristocracy rich enough to afford them, but for those sections of society with more limited resources the next best thing was paste. Antique paste was formed by heating a compound of crushed flint, lead oxide and potash. This formula was 'invented' by a jeweller from Strasbourg called Georges Frédéric Strass (1701-1773) who discovered that the addition of lead produced glass with a soft, diamond-like brilliance eminently suitable for faceting into gem replicas. Soon paste became a versatile and socially acceptable substitute for precious gems in which the gold and silver settings were of a comparable quality to those used in 'real' jewellery but at a fraction of the price.

Cheap and practical jewels and accessories were a notable feature of the 18th century, anticipating the huge demand for inexpensive bijouterie which was so much a feature of jewellery in the Victorian era. Christopher Pinchbeck (1672-1732), a Fleet Street watchmaker, discovered a method of combining copper and zinc to produce an alloy which was an effective simulant of gold. A plausible way of mounting inexpensive jewellery and accessories such as buckles and chatelaines, *pinchbeck* sold in large quantities up to the 19th century when it was gradually overtaken by poorer quality gilt metal. In 1762 Matthew Boulton (1728-1809), a steam engine manufacturer, perfected a

English diamond hexafoil flower brooch c.1775-1785. These lovely jewels were invariably pavé diamond set and fully enclosed at the back in silver. The smaller flower in the centre of this example is mounted en tremblant *on a coiled spring.* Woolley & Wallis

technique for faceting little studs of steel and setting them on to metal backplates. Comparable with diamonds in artificial light, dark grey *cut steel* was not exactly cheap but it certainly was an adaptable decoration for all manner of jewels and everyday objects in England and also in France. Another base material, not entirely dissimilar from cut steel, was *marcasite,* usually associated with 20th century costume jewellery. Georgian marcasite proved to be a perfectly acceptable diamond simulant. Cut and faceted from brassy yellow coloured iron pyrites (fool's gold), marcasite was effective when set in the borders of royal blue glass dress rings, Wedgwood jasper cameo brooches or painted miniatures where diamonds or pearls would have been simply too expensive.

Ornate dress jewellery such as girandole brooches and earrings, much beloved of the Spanish and French aristocracy, persisted in popularity right up to the end of the century. Indeed, in Spain and Portugal the fashion for extravagantly long and ornate silver and gold earrings set with unusual gems such as hessonite garnet or pale green chrysolites had never really lost their appeal over the preceding two hundred years. Nevertheless, by the 1790s and 1800s taste and fashion was visibly changing from over-complicated 'rocaille' embellishment to a minimal 'uncluttered' look of French inspiration known as *'Neo-classicism.'*

Rings, for example, became strongly visual where the bezel was fashioned into an elongated marquise (torpedo shape), a plain oval or a broad rectangular plaque with cut corners. Better quality examples were royal blue enamelled and studded with diamonds in cluster or floral spray formation, whilst memorial rings were painted with a miniature of a lady weeping tragically beside a tomb with an appropriate message of sentiment and a scattering of tiny pearls representing tears.

The classic English brooch of the 1780s and 1790s was the open flower, composed of six uniform-sized petals pavé set with rose-cut or 'old-mine' brilliant-cut diamonds while the Georgian collet rivière, composed of a line of graduated cushion-shaped gold and silver collets each set with a diamond, coloured gem or paste is probably one of the least complicated but most effective designs encountered in antique jewellery.

The classical influence was most powerfully portrayed in rings, brooches and necklaces mounted in 'Roman' gold seal settings. Here, a hardstone or shell cameo would be mounted in a thin rim of gold and set as a ring between broad 'trumpet'-shaped shoulders while necklaces composed of a series of cameos or colourful hardstone intaglios, some contemporary Georgian and some Roman, were joined together by three or four rows of fine link gold chain known as *en esclavage* swags. The key element was simplicity. Neo-classicism extended well into the 19th century and was clearly the dominant theme during the First Empire of Napoleonic France until it was gradually superseded by the richness and colour of the 1820s and 1830s.

Further reading

Jewellery in Britain 1066-1837, Diana Scarisbrick (Michael Russell Publishing Ltd)

Tudor and Jacobean Jewellery, Diana Scarisbrick (Tate Publishing)

Jewels and Jewellery, Clare Phillips (Victoria & Albert Museum)

A History of Jewellery 1100-1970, Joan Evans (Faber & Faber)

Jewelry from Antiquity to the Present, Clare Phillips (Thames & Hudson)

CHAPTER 3

A 19TH CENTURY JEWELLERY PANORAMA

An era which stretched from Napoleonic neo-classicism to late Victorian mechanisation and which encountered a breathtaking number of twists and turns along the way can be a little difficult to categorise. Nevertheless, it is possible to break the 19th century down into four distinct phases which broadly embrace the spectrum of jewellery design in a century of creative and restless change.

1800-1837 – Georgian Jewellery, William IV and the Napoleonic Legacy

There is a tendency today to pigeonhole as 'Regency' any item of English jewellery which vaguely appears to have been made during the first three decades of the 19th century. The fact is that three kings reigned during this period and jewellery design constantly evolved, particularly during the fifteen years leading up to Victoria's accession in 1837.

The years 1800 to 1810 are closely associated with neo-classicism, a style actively encouraged by Napoleon whose influence was all-consuming in the world of fashion and fine art during this time. Not that much jewellery had actually been made during the turbulent years of the French Revolution; diamond tiaras and necklaces were seen as un-acceptably bourgeois and contradicted every revolutionary principle. Sadly, much of the jewellery

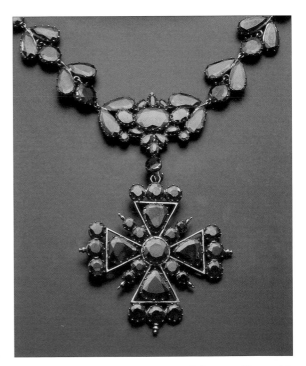

(Above) Early 19th century garnet foliate necklace with matching Maltese cross brooch/pendant mounted in gold.
S.J. Phillips

(Top) Cannetille gold and multi gem-set diadem brooch c.1830. All the stones are individually foiled to intensify their brilliance.
S.J. Phillips

White chalcedony, cannetille gold and gem-set cruciform pendant c.1830. Pink topaz and turquoise were favourite gems in these pretty jewels; the centre opens to reveal a compartment for a lock of hair.

owned by the aristocracy at the end of the 18th century was simply broken up and sold.

Napoleon's campaigns in Egypt and Italy inspired jewellery which was clearly influenced by the art and treasure of the Ancients. By the early 1800s elaborate gold tiaras, armbands and clasps were set with imposing hardstone or shell cameos, carved to depict mythological deities and classical groups. Sometimes these materials – particularly the intaglios – were genuine, excavated ancient artefacts. To reinforce the classical ideal, settings were fashioned in gold in the design of laurel wreaths, palmettes and Greek keys. Another popular 'classical' medium was the mosaic in which tiny pieces of coloured glass were carefully grouped together to form a picture such as a landscape or architectural ruin. These mosaic plaques were then mounted in thin gold frames and fashioned as necklaces and bracelets with fine-link gold chain 'swags' in between.

Naturalism – flowers, sprays, leaves and wreaths – dominated Georgian diamond jewellery with heavy closed-back silver settings gradually giving way to lighter open-back mounts in gold by the 1830s. Indeed, gold suddenly became the focal point of jewellery design with the appearance of the *cannetille frame* – elaborate gold wire decoration similar to filigree work. Cannetille was the perfect accompaniment for foil-back pastel colour gemstones such as aquamarine, pink topaz, chrysolite and pale amethyst or subtle hardstones such as white chalcedony or pale green chrysoprase. By the 1830s complete suites of gem-set cannetille jewels known as *parures* were fashionable in both Paris and London. Comprising necklace, bracelets, earrings and a matching girandole brooch, the individual gems were usually foiled to accentuate both colour and sparkle.

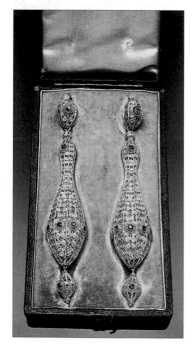

This pair of exquisite gold filigree and garnet lantern drop earrings are in their original fitted case with a jeweller's label 'E & W Smith Goldsmith & Jewellers to His Majesty & His Royal Highness The Duke of York'. The earrings can thus be dated to between 1820 and 1827.
Woolley & Wallis

Fine Georgian gold belcher link muff chain c.1825. These chains are remorselessly copied today although modern examples are heavier and cruder than the originals. Note the characteristic 'star' decoration and jewelled hand clasp.
S.J. Phillips

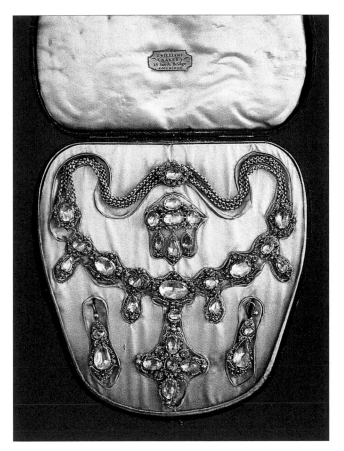

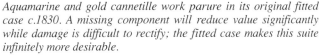

Aquamarine and gold cannetille work parure in its original fitted case c.1830. A missing component will reduce value significantly while damage is difficult to rectify; the fitted case makes this suite infinitely more desirable.

Victorian seed pearl brooch c.1850. Seed pearl jewellery is fairly inexpensive due to its tendency to fall apart.

The 1830s are also associated with the passion for sentimentality in which messages were conveyed in a little brooch or ring set with a line of coloured gems spelling a name or appropriate endearment such as 'Dearest' or 'Regard.' The frames of many of these sentimental jewels – padlocks, keys and hearts – or accessories such as fob seals and watch keys were richly decorated in several different colours of gold which were then embellished with floral carving and set with little gems such as ruby or turquoise. So-called 'trois couleur' or 'quatre couleur' gold was achieved by adding minute quantities of other metals such as copper (red gold), silver (green gold) or nickel (white gold).

1837-1860 – Early Victorian Romanticism

This elegant era was also the period of greatest change in jewellery development and symbolism. In the 1840s naturalism continued to influence with realistic and intricate seed pearl and gold brooches fashioned as clusters of grapes, seed pearls woven into necklaces and brooches on mother-of-pearl backplates and bows, tendrils, leaves and straps finely wrought in gold, chased with tiny flowers and scrolls and decorated with pretty shades of opaque enamel, particularly sky blue and navy. Bracelets were possibly the most popular type of jewel in the 1840s and 1850s; straps of adjustable length with jewelled buckles and bangles of 'Algerian Knot'

(Above) Gold and almandine garnet knot brooch, 1850.

(Right) Gold brooch with tassel fringe and sphere drop c.1860-70. Such brooches invariably contained a compartment at the back for a lock of hair.

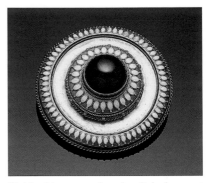

Gold white enamel and polished garnet cabochon locket-back brooch, English c.1860. This type of brooch was common in the mid-Victorian period; other popular materials included turquoise, onyx and sky-blue enamel decorated with diamonds and half pearls. Wimpole Antiques

design were characteristic of the period. The 1840s also saw the development of the serpent necklace and bracelet. These cobra-like snakes were enamelled and set with diamonds, precious gems or a richly-coloured stone such as a garnet in the head. A heart-shaped locket back drop was invariably suspended from the serpent's mouth concealing a plume of hair.

Mourning jewellery perfectly articulated the fashion for sentiment at this time with brooches in gilt metal and gold containing hair in chased gold mounts. The jet industry flourished, located at Whitby in North Yorkshire. Ultimately two hundred workshops prospered in Whitby alone, barely keeping pace with the country's obsession for mourning after the death of Prince Albert in 1861.

Italian mosaic jewellery persisted in popularity although the quality of much of this later material is noticeably coarser than the tiny tesserae pieces used in early 19th century mosaic jewellery. By the 1850s and 1860s the tourist industry was in full swing and visitors to Rome, Florence, Naples and the ruins at Pompeii began to bring back souvenirs of their visits. Cameos carved from a wide range of materials were fashioned locally and mounted in bright yellow gold frames. Shell and coral from Naples proved to be the ideal media for designs which ranged from classical female deities to severe Victorian gentlemen, while volcanic lava from Mount Vesuvius was carved into cameos of prominent figures in history such as Michelangelo and Shakespeare. Coral was a particular favourite at this time, fashioned into an amazing array of imaginative shapes from simple faceted tear-drops to tortured sea-serpents and grotesques. Sometimes the coral branches were wrought into brooches and tiaras, capped in gold and embellished with little coral beads with the appearance of berries. Other gems in

Pavé set turquoise and gold snake necklace with garnet eyes and diamond jaws, c.1845. Bentley & Skinner

fashion in the 1850s included turquoise, pavé-set in cluster formation, and rich, deep red pyrope garnet polished into domed cabochons and mounted in diamond and enamel naturalistic frames.

1860-1880 – Mid Victorian Confidence and Revivalism

The era of exploration, prosperity and endeavour, the 1860s and 1870s were a period dominated by jewellery of historical inspiration. During this time, the all-consuming passion for 'archaeological' gold jewels became something of a European obsession while enormous interest in the art and iconography of the Renaissance resulted in many extremely colourful designs in which enamel played just as important a role as gemstones.

The fashion for neo-classical revivalism which had been so active in the early 1800s was given new life and impetus by a group of Italian goldsmiths of which the most celebrated was Fortunato Pio Castellani. Pioneering the technique of applying minute shot-work motifs to a gold surface, Castellani managed to revive a skill which had died out with the ancient Etruscans. To reinforce the absolute integrity of their work, Castellani and his contemporaries chose to use ancient materials – Egyptian hardstone scarabs and Roman silver coins in fine yellow gold settings crowded with academic symbolism such as acanthus leaves, fibulae, amphorae and sphinxes.

By the 1860s gemstone polishing had advanced to the extent that colourful stones such as garnet, coral and turquoise could be cut and shaped to fit the contours of a setting. Turquoises, for example, were polished into pyramids and closely set into the covers of oval gold lockets with little diamonds studded in between. Sometimes the gems themselves were chiselled and set with a diamond star or naturalistic motif such as a flower or even a jewelled insect. By the 1870s pendants and brooches were mounted with striking, deep red garnet cabochons, diamonds and pale green chrysolites in complicated multi-coloured champlevé enamel frames. Inspired by Renaissance art, these extremely pretty pieces were known as *Holbeinesque* jewels.

Interest in Neo-Renaissance jewellery became as

Turquoise and rose diamond heart-shaped gold locket c.1875. The turquoises have been individually polished and shaped to form an effective geometric pattern.

compelling as classical revivalism in the 1870s. Goldsmiths such as Carlo Giuliano and Robert Phillips produced vibrant and highly colourful enamelled jewels mounted with compatible hardstones and simple polished semi-precious gems which reinforced the sense of 'Tudor' realism while a demand for technically superior gold jewellery wrought into designs inspired by Gothic symbolism – grotesques, masks and fierce dragons known as *broches-chimères* – became highly fashionable in France and Germany.

In Paris Alexis Falize, in collaboration with the celebrated enameller Tard, executed cloisonné enamel lockets and pendants in the 'Japanese taste'

Broad 15 carat gold cuff bangle with 'Assyrian' wirework decoration c.1860-70.   Author's Collection

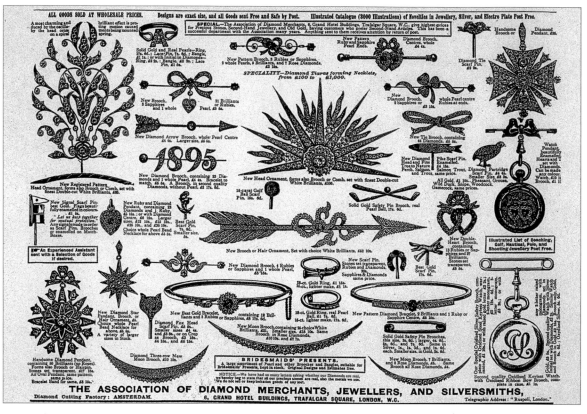

Extract from The Graphic *27 July 1895 illustrating a number of affordable and pretty jewels popular at the time.*

and Nature continued to fascinate the market with insect brooches – houseflies, bees and spiders – as popular as jewellery fashioned from the body plates of the hawksbill turtle, better known as tortoiseshell piqué work. In India tigers were shot and their claws were mounted in gold cap settings to be worn in rather hideous parures. Hummingbird heads were mounted in gold brooches, scarab beetles as necklaces and strange lid-like filters from fish known as operculum shells were grouped into livid parures. The 1870s was decidedly the decade in which wildlife – both real and artificial – played a dominant role in decorative jewellery design.

1880-1901 – Late Victorian Mass Production

It is difficult today to conceive the sheer quantity of cheap, versatile and wearable jewellery which was pumped out to sustain the demands of a near-insatiable market during the 1880s and 1890s.

For those who could afford them, diamonds were abundant and readily available, sourced from the recently discovered fields located at Kimberley in South Africa. Coloured stones – especially ruby, sapphire, turquoise and opal – were traded by international gem merchants while deposits of gold and silver were discovered and extracted from sites as far flung as Australia and North America. This was the era of prosperity, economic growth and confidence in which a burgeoning middle class possessed the disposable income to afford a diamond ring, a star brooch or even an opulent tiara readily available from a blossoming number of jewellery shops situated in most large and medium sized towns up and down the British Isles. 'Everyday' jewellery – gold chains, sentimental brooches, curb link bracelets and a bottomless pit of simple gold rings set with small but effective precious gems – comprised the cheap but crucial 'bread and butter' sales at the bottom end of the market, sourced from a network of small jewellery workshops located in Birmingham, Sheffield and London.

Much of this output was of distinctly average quality and does not bear close scrutiny. Gems such as ruby, emerald and sapphire could be heavily flawed and inferior of colour while much of the nine carat gold jewellery, including bangles, rings and brooches, was set with paste simulants or doublets – composition stones which looked like the real thing but which were intended to deceive.

Nine carat gold was indeed a basic and plentiful material used in the production of jewellery for the masses. Composed of three parts gold and five parts base metal, it was inexpensive and robust and soon became the ideal medium for heavy wearing accessories such as cufflinks, pocket watches and alberts or more decorative items such as hollow locket-back brooches and guard chains. The addition of copper resulted in rose gold, a tint which was particularly favoured in curb link bracelets and watch chains. Fifteen carat and eighteen carat were reserved for better quality gem-set jewels of a decidedly superior design and finish.

One of the most influential goldsmiths active at the end of the 19th century was Edwin Streeter, whose business established at 18 New Bond Street supplied a broad and varied range of diamond and gem-set jewellery and accessories (see pages 60 and 61). Alongside practical and conventional engagement rings and half hoop bangles, much of Streeter's stock clearly catered for a strongly sentimental public for which rings and brooches were designed as hearts, bows, lovers' knots, horseshoes and shamrocks. Sport and recreational activities were also performing an increasingly influential part in people's lives at the end of the Victorian era. Leisure pursuits such as golf, fishing, cycling, hunting and horse racing resulted in a plethora of novelty brooches and tiepins set with diamonds or decorated in enamel such as bicycles with revolving wheels, golf club bar brooches with pearl 'balls', galloping racehorse brooches with enamel jockeys and even diamond violins.

Victorian gold ring gipsy-set with emeralds and diamonds c.1900. Woolley & Wallis

Victorian gold double snake ring set with two old-mine cut diamonds c.1880. Woolley & Wallis

'The Classic' late Victorian graduated five-stone diamond half hoop ring. Invariably mounted in a carved gold scrolling gallery, tiny rose diamond 'points' were set in between the principal stones. Woolley & Wallis

Another half hoop set with sapphires and diamonds. Woolley & Wallis

Sapphire and diamond cluster ring on a broad 18 carat old mount c.1885. Woolley & Wallis

Summary of Jewellery Designs Fashionable from the 1880s to the early 1900s

Rings

'Half hoop' gold bands with carved scrolling galleries set in silver with a line of three, five or more diamonds or coloured gems, notably sapphire, ruby, half pearl, coral, turquoise or opal.

Broad, polished gold hoops 'gipsy-set' with a single diamond or native-cut gem. Cluster rings composed of a principal centre stone in a surround of eight or twelve smaller gems.

'Crossover' rings incorporating two or more stones set in oblique formation on a waved mount. Sentimental 'heart and coronet' rings in open-back gold and silver settings.

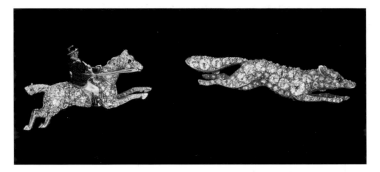

Pavé diamond set running fox brooch c.1890 together with a brooch modelled as an enamelled huntsman on a diamond horse. These beautifully modelled brooches deftly tapped into the great passion for hunting and other recreational activities popular at the time such as cycling, fishing and golf. Bentley & Skinner

Diamond pavé-set racehorse brooch and a similarly set foxhead brooch c.1890.

Brooches

Late Victorian 'primary' brooches, i.e. those set with diamonds and coloured stones such as sapphires and rubies, were mounted in gold and set in cut down silver collets. Settings were invariably embellished with small rose-cut diamonds. Crescent brooches, for example, were set with a line of graduated cushion-shaped gems with tiny rose diamond endstones. Many standard designs such as sunbursts, stars and flower sprays were accompanied by a tortoiseshell comb which would be screwed into the back of the brooch mount once the pin had been removed.

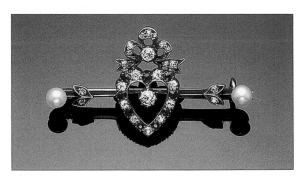

Gold line brooch with ruby and diamond heart surmount and pearl finials c.1895. Woolley & Wallis

English 15 carat gold, half pearl and diamond lozenge brooch c.1885. Simple plaque and bar brooches were incredibly common at the end of the 19th century with large numbers in 9 carat gold set with cheap – and very basic – gems such as garnet, peridot and paste.

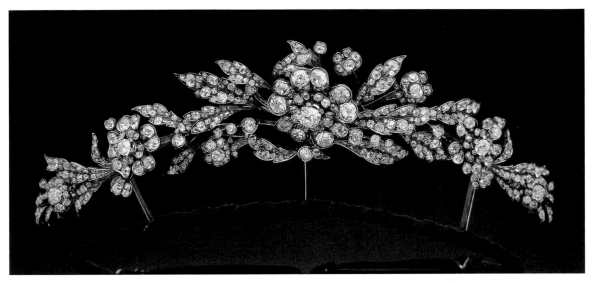

English diamond flower spray tiara c.1880. In common with most Victorian tiaras and diadems, the clusters can be separately dismantled for conversion into a series of brooches. A box with all the original fittings is thus an advantage.
Woolley & Wallis

Primary Brooch Designs

'Celestial' themes including diamond stars, sunbursts and crescent moons in open and closed formation.

Flower sprays, cascades, daisy clusters and leaves.

Tied bows and wavy ribbons.

Target clusters and diamond horseshoes.

Butterflies set with diamonds and contrasting lines of rubies, sapphires and pearls.

Dragonflies in which the wings were mounted with shaped panels of gemstones such as opal and amethyst.

Lizards which were often set with opals, emeralds or demantoid garnets.

(Right above) English diamond wheatsheaf and flower brooch c.1890. Woolley & Wallis

(Right) Diamond star brooch c.1890. Together with crescents and flower sprays, stars are among the most common of Victorian brooch designs. Many examples have been rhodium plated to create a more 'modern' look, a factor which can reduce their appeal. Woolley & Wallis

Oriental pearl and diamond cluster necklace with similarly set earrings c.1900. Pearls and diamonds were a popular combination at the end of the century. Typically, the settings are a combination of both silver and gold.
Woolley & Wallis

Diamond flower spray brooch, probably Turkish c.1890. Eastern European and Oriental 19th century jewellery can often be rather crude such as in this example set with foil-back 'lasqué' cut diamonds.

Novelty Brooch Designs
Include a wide range of sporting and recreational themes from golf and fishing to domestic pets, musical instruments, locomotives and even necrophilia in the form of enamelled 'skull' tiepins.

Secondary Brooch Designs
This category includes the vast majority of simple nine and fifteen carat gold decorative brooches which were invariably set with half pearls and a colourful gemstone such as garnet, amethyst, aquamarine or peridot. Designs ranged from basic scrolls, clusters, shamrocks and stars to rather more elaborate sprays fashioned as swallows in flight, lily of the valley or wild rose set with half pearls or decorated with small gems and enamel.

Sentimental themes such as two hearts entwined, lovers' knots and horseshoes.

Insects, especially spiders, flies and beetles, mounted on a simple gold bar.

Safety bar brooches incorporating a line of matching semi-precious gems or a small single diamond.

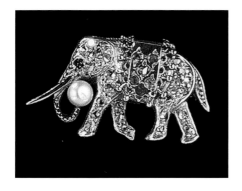

(Far left) Diamond and gem-set novelty brooch in the design of an elephant c.1895. Bentley & Skinner

(Left) Late Victorian novelty insect brooch. The imaginative use of diamonds and colourful gems makes these 'bug brooches' very collectable. Woolley & Wallis

Lockets and Pendants

Lockets were particularly popular in the 1880s and 1890s ranging from large and ornate examples in silver or gold which were worn from compatible collars to small circular, oval and heart-shaped lockets with gold 'fronts and backs' and metal linings. Many lockets were engraved with a message of sentiment such as 'regard' or were inscribed with the owner's monogram. Mid-size gold lockets were often embellished with a gem-set star or double horseshoe surmount, while expensive examples were pavé-set with half pearls, diamonds or turquoises. A classic of the time was the heart-shaped pavé diamond locket with a hinged rock crystal back cover. Inexpensive but effective materials used included jet, bog oak, ivory, gilt metal and gunmetal.

Pendants often conformed to the naturalistic scrolling designs of brooches and were set with the 'standard' gems of the day, half pearl, garnet, aquamarine and peridot being particularly common. A striking example of turn of the century jewellery was the negligée pendant in which two gems or clusters were suspended by bars or chains of unequal length from a matching top.

Three turn of the century gem-set half pearl brooch/pendants. Pretty and versatile, the majority of these colourful little jewels were mounted in 9 carat gold. Popular gems included peridot, garnet and aquamarine. Cheap copies were set with imitation pearls and pastes. Sylvie Spectrum

English gold locket c.1880 profusely engraved and bearing the motto 'Regard.' A prime example of sentimental jewellery popular at the time.

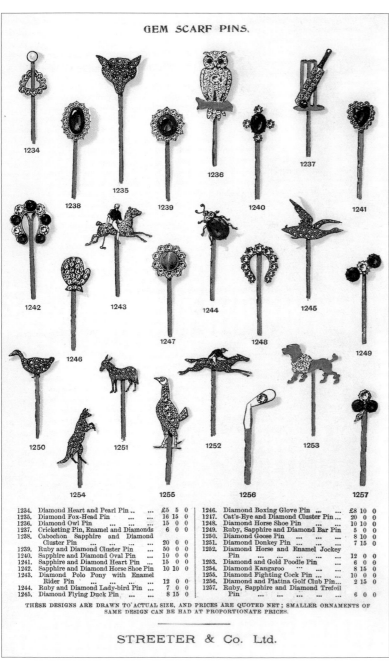

GEM SCARF PINS.

1234.	Diamond Heart and Pearl Pin	£5	5	0
1235.	Diamond Fox-Head Pin	16 15	0
1236.	Diamond Owl Pin	15	0	0
1237.	Cricketing Pin, Enamel and Diamonds	6	0	0
1238.	Cabochon Sapphire and Diamond Cluster Pin	20	0	0
1239.	Ruby and Diamond Cluster Pin ...	50	0	0
1240.	Sapphire and Diamond Oval Pin ...	10	0	0
1241.	Sapphire and Diamond Heart Pin ...	15	0	0
1242.	Sapphire and Diamond Horse Shoe Pin	10 10	0
1243.	Diamond Polo Pony with Enamel Rider Pin	12	0	0
1244.	Ruby and Diamond Lady-bird Pin ...	7	0	0
1245.	Diamond Flying Duck Pin	8 15	0
1246.	Diamond Boxing Glove Pin	£8 10	0
1247.	Cat's-Eye and Diamond Cluster Pin ...	20	0	0
1248.	Diamond Horse Shoe Pin	10 10	0
1249.	Ruby, Sapphire and Diamond Bar Pin	5	0	0
1250.	Diamond Goose Pin	8 10	0
1251.	Diamond Donkey Pin	7 15	0
1252.	Diamond Horse and Enamel Jockey Pin	12	0	0
1253.	Diamond and Gold Poodle Pin ...	6	0	0
1254.	Diamond Kangaroo	8 15	0
1255.	Diamond Fighting Cock Pin	10	0	0
1256.	Diamond and Platina Golf Club Pin...	2 15	0
1257.	Ruby, Sapphire and Diamond Trefoil Pin	6	0	0

THESE DESIGNS ARE DRAWN TO ACTUAL SIZE, AND PRICES ARE QUOTED NET; SMALLER ORNAMENTS OF SAME DESIGN CAN BE HAD AT PROPORTIONATE PRICES.

STREETER & Co. Ltd.

Six pages from Gems *by Edwin W. Streeter, London, c.1898.*

GEM BRACELETS. 25

1111.	Diamond Snaffle Bit and Horse Shoe on Gold Curb Bracelet	£42 10	0
1112.	Cat's-eye and Diamond Three-Cluster on Gold Curb Bracelet ...	35	0	0
1113.	Sapphire and Diamond Scroll and Gold Curb Bracelet ...	45	0	0
1114.	Pearl and Diamond alternate on Gold Curb Bracelet ...	35	0	0
1115.	Turquoise and Diamond Fancy Flexible Bracelet	50	0	0
1116.	Diamond Heart and Cluster Flexible Bracelet	150	0	0
1117.	Ruby and Diamond alternate on Gold Curb Bracelet	26	0	0
1118.	Opal and Diamond Heart and Tie Bracelet	28	0	0
1119.	Pearl and Diamond Collet on Gold Curb Bracelet	65	0	0

THESE DESIGNS ARE DRAWN TO ACTUAL SIZE, AND PRICES ARE QUOTED NET; SMALLER ORNAMENTS OF SAME DESIGN CAN BE HAD AT PROPORTIONATE PRICES.

18, New Bond Street, W.

DIAMOND NECKLACES and EARRINGS. 27

1129. 1130. 1131.	Fine Diamond Riviere Necklaces, from £100 upwards, according to size.		
1132. 1133. 1134. 1135. 1136.	Fine Diamond Single Stone Earrings, from £20 upwards, according to size.		
1137.	Pair Pearl and Diamond Cluster Earrings ...	£35	0	0
1138.	Pair Turquoise and Diamond Cluster Earrings ...	50	0	0
1139.	Pair Sapphire and Diamond Cluster Earrings ...	30	0	0

THESE DESIGNS ARE DRAWN TO ACTUAL SIZE, AND PRICES ARE QUOTED NET; SMALLER ORNAMENTS OF SAME DESIGN CAN BE HAD AT PROPORTIONATE PRICES.

18, New Bond Street, W.

The £10 10s. Jewel page. 19

		£	s.	d.
1026.	Sapphire and Diamond Double Heart and Coronet Brooch ...	£10	10	0
1027.	Diamond Heart with Enamel (any color) Slipper Brooch ...	10	10	0
1028.	Diamond Tie Brooch	10	10	0
1029.	Diamond Fancy Heart Brooch	10	10	0
1030.	Turquoise and Diamond Heart Pendant	10	10	0
1031.	Cabochon Ruby and Diamond on Gold Curb Bracelet ...	10	10	0
1032.	Opal and Diamond Heart Pendant...	10	10	0
1033.	Opal and Diamond Fancy Pendant	10	10	0
1034.	Sapphires and Diamonds on Gold Curb Bracelet ...	10	10	0
1035.	Jade Shamrock and Diamond Heart Pendant ...	10	10	0
1036.	Turquoise Three-Stone Ring	10	10	0
1037.	All Diamond Trefoil Ring	10	10	0
1038.	Cabochon Ruby and Diamond Heart Ring ...	10	10	0
1039.	Ruby and Diamond Twisted Front Bracelet ...	10	10	0
1040.	Opal and Diamond Double Part Ring	10	10	0
1041.	Ruby and Diamond Bangle Ring	10	10	0
1042.	Opal and Diamond Cluster Bracelet	10	10	0
1043.	Opal and Diamond Marquise Ring	10	10	0

THESE DESIGNS ARE DRAWN TO ACTUAL SIZE, AND PRICES ARE QUOTED NET; SMALLER ORNAMENTS OF SAME DESIGN CAN BE HAD AT PROPORTIONATE PRICES.

18, New Bond Street, W.

22 SPORTING MODELS, mounted in Diamonds.

		£	s.	d.
1074.	Diamond Pomeranian Dog Brooch	£25	0	0
1075.	Diamond Deer Brooch	22	0	0
1076.	Diamond Dachshund Brooch	22	0	0
1077.	Diamond Hackney Brooch	25	0	0
1078.	Diamond Otter Brooch	33	0	0
1079.	Diamond Woodcock Brooch	41	10	0
1080.	Diamond and Enamel Golf Player Brooch ...	15	0	0
1081.	Diamond Bicycle Brooch	20	0	0
1082.	Diamond Owl Brooch	23	0	0
1083.	Diamond Donkey Brooch	35	0	0
1084.	Diamond Lucky Pig Brooch	45	0	0
1085.	Diamond Running Fox Brooch	30	0	0
1086.	Diamond Polo Pony with Enamel Rider Brooch ...	25	0	0
1087.	Diamond and Enamel Hansom Cab Brooch ...	12	0	0
1088.	Diamond Collie Dog Brooch	33	0	0

THESE DESIGNS ARE DRAWN TO ACTUAL SIZE, AND PRICES ARE QUOTED NET; SMALLER ORNAMENTS OF SAME DESIGN CAN BE HAD AT PROPORTIONATE PRICES.

GEM BROOCHES. 21

		£	s.	d.
1059.	Sapphire and Diamond Cluster Brooch	£100	0	0
1060.	Diamond Butterfly Brooch	110	0	0
1061.	Colored Pearl and Diamond Four Leaf Shamrock Brooch ...	85	0	0
1062.	Diamond Antique Pattern Brooch	60	0	0
1063.	Ruby and Diamond Double Row Crescent Brooch ...	45	0	0
1064.	Diamond Crescent and Comet Brooch	34	0	0
1065.	Diamond Antique Brooch...	25	0	0
1066.	Pearl and Diamond Spider and Web Brooch (half size £20)	35	0	0
1067.	Pink, Black and White Pearl and Diamond Brooch ...	40	0	0
1068.	Pearl and Diamond Twist Knot Brooch ...	18	0	0
1069.	Sapphire and Diamond Half-Moon Brooch ...	35	0	0
1070.	Ruby and Diamond Horse Shoe Brooch ...	40	0	0
1071.	Opal and Diamond Heart on Bar Brooch ...	15	0	0
1072.	Opal and Diamond Fancy Bar Brooch ...	12	10	0
1073.	Opal and Diamond Fancy Bar Brooch ...	6	15	0

THESE DESIGNS ARE DRAWN TO ACTUAL SIZE, AND PRICES ARE QUOTED NET; SMALLER ORNAMENTS OF SAME DESIGN CAN BE HAD AT PROPORTIONATE PRICES.

18, New Bond Street, W.

(Far left) Turquoise and half pearl flower link necklace c.1895. Woolley & Wallis

(Left) 15 carat gold and pearl floral necklace with detachable heart pendant c.1895. Woolley & Wallis

Necklaces

The late 19th century was the era of the diamond rivière – a line of some thirty or forty matching graduated brilliant-cut diamonds or gemstones in simple cut-down collet settings. Diamonds were extremely plentiful and were set in somewhat repetitive designs such as the fringe necklace – a series of graduated spear, floral cluster or tear-shaped drops with knife-edge bars connecting to a diamond gallery above.

Secondary necklaces repeated this theme with fringes of drop-shaped amethyst, moonstone, garnet, peridot and citrine mounted in either silver or gold. Pearl-set fifteen carat gold necklaces were both common and easy to wear and many still survive today. 9 carat gold necklaces were often 'spectacle set' with a line of cheap semi-precious gems while Indian amethyst, ruby and citrine necklaces formed a graduated tier below a gallery of woven seed pearls. Gold and silver chains were also worn at the end of the 19th century. The majority of nine carat guard chains contained 'secret' links for strength and protection against wear, while chains were sometimes worn together with a fob watch, a locket or an embossed seal.

Earrings

Largely confined to the same designs used for rings such as a single diamond stud or a floral cluster of diamonds encircling a coloured gemstone or diamond to the centre.

Bangles and Bracelets

Designs were broadly similar to rings such as a line of diamonds or gems in 'half hoop' graduated formation. A plain gold hoop bangle was invariably hinged at the side and mounted to the centre with a decorative device such as a flower, a horseshoe or two entwined hearts. Inexpensive nine carat gold models were fashionably set with cheap composition gems and rose diamond chips while broad gold and silver cuff bangles were profusely decorated with flowers, birds and scrolls or fashioned into the design of buckles and straps.

Bracelets, commonly of continuous curb link designs, were studded with gems such as turquoise, half pearl, opal and amethyst. Russian bracelets from this period were sometimes composed of a combination of fourteen carat red, white and yellow gold links and suspended below pendants such as miniature eggs or religious charms.

A pair of Late Victorian cushion-shaped old-mine cut diamonds remounted as earrings in the 1950s. Woolley & Wallis

A pair of Oriental pearl and diamond pendant earrings c.1890. Woolley & Wallis

Further reading

Understanding Jewellery, David Bennett and Daniela Mascetti (Antique Collectors' Club)

The Art of the Jeweller: A Catalogue of the Hull Grundy Gift to the British Museum (British Museum Publications Ltd.)

English Victorian Jewellery, Ernle Bradford (Country Life)

Victorian Jewellery, Margaret Flower (Cassell)

Antique and 20th Century Jewellery, Vivienne Becker (NAG Press)

(Above) Victorian sapphire and diamond hinged gold crossover bangle c.1895. Woolley & Wallis

(Above left) Diamond hinged gold bangle c.1885. So-called 'triple hoop' designs made equally effective dress rings which might combine lines of rubies, sapphires and diamonds representing the colours of the Union flag. Woolley & Wallis

(Right) Oriental pearl and diamond bangle c.1895. The pearls used in much late Victorian jewellery were of a flattened compressed shape known as boutons. Woolley & Wallis

Early 17th century enamelled brooch of the Annunciation in a later gold frame. A fine example of basse-taille *enamelling in which brilliant translucent colours are applied to a gold or silver ground in low relief.*　Sandra Cronan

George and the Dragon brooch c.1630. Opaque white enamel was usually termed email en blanc. *Another example is illustrated on page 42 (centre).*　Sandra Cronan

CHAPTER 4

ENAMELS

Enamel is a combination of glass silicate and powdered metallic oxide fused on to a metallic surface by heating at high intensity in a furnace. Versatile, decorative and visually enriching, enamel can be just as effective when used exclusively as when accompanied by diamonds or gems. Indeed, during the 16th and 17th centuries, enamel invariably took the place of gemstones which were hard to obtain, expensive and difficult to cut and polish.

Enamel was widely used in 19th century jewellery,

Sixteenth century enamel gem-set figurative gold ring c.1550-1600. The technique of enamelling figures 'in the round' was known as encrusted enamelling or émail en ronde bosse.

either exclusively as a decorative embellishment to mid-Victorian naturalistic gold pendants, bracelets and brooches or as a further decoration to gem-set pieces such as snake necklaces and bangles, where blue enamel was the ideal accompaniment for diamonds, rubies and half pearls. Coral jewellery was often lifted by a splash of green or blue enamel and black enamel is so closely associated with mourning jewellery that it is nearly impossible to associate the colour with anything else.

From a purely technical point of view the medium probably reached its zenith during the early part of the last century when Fabergé, Cartier and Art Nouveau goldsmiths such as Lalique took their own enamelling techniques to levels of excellence never seen before.

There are several methods of enamelling which were fairly common in the Middle Ages but which are so rarely seen today as to render them academic. The more common varieties encountered in antique jewellery are as follows:

Cambridge blue enamel, half pearl and diamond pendant c.1865-1870. Here, the star has been 'sunk' into the surrounding enamel. Such pieces were often accompanied by a matching bangle or earrings.

Champlevé enamel 'Holbeinesque' pendant mounted with garnet cabochons and chrysolites c.1875. These Renaissance-style jewels were invariably engraved on the back with a profusion of flowers.

Fine royal blue painted enamel and diamond com-memorative jewel celebrating George IV's coronation in 1820.

Cloisonné Enamelling

Thin strips of wire – gold, silver or metal – are soldered to the surface of a metal object and are shaped into individual decorative 'cells' known as cloisons. Each cell is filled with powdered enamel which is then fired and polished when cool. Cloisonné enamel was used in China and Japan on large scale objects such as vases whilst the technique was revived by the French goldsmith Alexis Falize (1811-1898) and his son Lucien (1838-1897) in colourful gold pendants, lockets and bracelets depicting animals, birds and flowers in the Oriental taste.

Champlevé Enamelling

The opposite of cloisonné; the metal surface of an object was hollowed out into cells forming individual patterns which were then filled with coloured enamel, fired and smoothed flat. A technique known since ancient times, champlevé was used to striking effect in 19th century Neo-Renaissance jewellery known as *Holbeinesque* in which colourful gemstones such as garnets and chrysolites were mounted in polychrome enamel frames.

Pair of gold buttons by the jewellers Falize decorated with cloisonné enamel birds in the Japanese taste, c.1870.

An Indian gold bracelet studded with a range of colourful gems and enamelled with foliate decoration. Indian enamelling is often highly elaborate and may depict a range of subjects such as elephants, peacocks and flowers. c.1800-1850.
Private Collection/Bridgeman Art Library

Cartier rock crystal mantel clock with translucent guilloché *enamel face within an opaque white enamel and gold chapter ring, c.1915. Like Fabergé, Cartier excelled in their application of coloured enamels to an engraved surface.*

En Plein Enamelling

Coating a relatively large area such as a cigarette case or photograph frame with several layers of enamel which have been individually fired and allowed to cool. Technically difficult, poor en plein enamelling exhibits an uneven surface and tiny air bubbles.

Guilloché Enamelling

Coats of transparent enamel covering a metal surface which has been finely engraved with a geometric pattern such as a 'sunburst' or 'watered silk'. This technique was mastered by Fabergé whose ability to create objects as small as a pair of cufflinks or as large as an Imperial Easter egg decorated with guilloché enamel was simply incomparable.

Painted Enamel

An early method, usually executed on copper. Layers of colour were individually built up and separately fired; designs were sometimes enhanced by metal foiling.

Counter Enamelling

Coating the back of an object with a layer of strengthening enamel. 17th century Dutch or English lockets were often counter enamelled in sky-blue.

Semi-translucent pink and green matt enamel and pearl flower pendant c.1880.
Bentley & Skinner

Painted enamel and table-cut diamond cross c.1650. English and Dutch enamel jewellery of this period was often counter enamelled *in sky blue or white on the back of the jewel.*

The vibrant colours of Limoges enamel meant that a large proportion of the subjects depicted were of Medieval or Renaissance inspiration such as Joan of Arc or a noblewoman in Tudor costume.

Swiss enamel and gold brooch c.1850. Tranquil scenes of Lake Geneva and maidens in national costume were typical of these early to mid-19th century souvenir brooches which were sometimes identified on the back of the plaques. Condition is absolutely critical since chips and cracks cannot be repaired. RBR Group at Grays

Swiss Enamel

Popular in 18th and 19th century brooches and bracelets, 'Geneva' enamel depicted Alpine landscapes or girls wearing the costume of their national Swiss canton. These portraits were highly proficient but care should be taken to ensure that examples are free of chips which reveal the copper background. Damaged Swiss enamel is impossible to restore.

Plique-à-jour Enamelling

An important technique which is closely associated with Art Nouveau jewellery. The individual cells do not have a metal backing so the light shines through when the object is held up to the light. The enamel therefore acts in much the same way as a stained glass window and was ideal for naturalistic pendants depicting colourful flowers or dragonfly brooches where shades of coloured plique-à-jour enamel filled the individual cells in the insect's wing.

Further reading

The Art of the Jeweller: A Catalogue of the Hull Grundy Gift to the British Museum (British Museum Publications Ltd.)

Jewellery – The International Era 1789-1910, Shirley Bury (Antique Collectors' Club)

Jewelry & Metalwork in the Arts and Crafts Tradition, Elyse Zorn Karlin (Schiffer Publishing Ltd.)

Highly colourful French plique-à-jour *enamel and diamond butterfly brooch c.1900.*

CHAPTER 5

'FALSE DIAMONDS'
PASTE JEWELLERY FROM THE 1750S TO THE 1930S

Antique paste – particularly the 19th century material – was one of those commodities which quite literally could be bought for next to nothing. Then, in the 1970s, M.D.S. Lewis' superb book on the subject brought paste to a wider audience and suddenly collectors were clamouring for pretty Georgian buttons, flower spray brooches and classical diadems which could previously be bought for well under £100. Today a 'Queen Anne' necklace of faceted paste collets foiled a desirable colour such as aquamarine blue or emerald green can easily sell for £2,000. Therein lies the great strength of fine old paste jewellery. Instead of mere copies of real diamonds and gems, it should be embraced for what it truly is: elegant, beautifully constructed jewels, marvellous to handle, versatile and enriching to wear and a perfect expression of the period in which it was constructed.

Glass had been extensively used in decorative ornamentation since ancient times. Roman rings, for example, were sometimes set with little, coloured glass plaques while brooch pins of Saxon origin were decorated with sections of glass or further embellished with enamel. Such glass was soft and fragile and wore down easily, often resulting in an abraded and unattractive lustre. It was not until the 17th century that an Englishman, George Ravenscroft, began experimenting with new compounds of flint, potash and lead oxide producing 'glass of lead', a lustrous material which proved sufficiently hard to cut and polish like a gemstone. However, it was the pioneering endeavours of Georges Frédéric Strass (1701-1773), a jeweller working in Paris, who fundamentally influenced the manner in which everyday jewellery was worn in the 18th century.

Like Ravenscroft, Strass experimented with lead crystal which could be faceted to imitate diamonds and which was mounted in silver settings to simulate genuine and costly alternatives. The key to Strass' success was to market his so-called 'false diamonds' to the French King and the Bourbon Court. Soon this new product became both fashionable and essential in a society fraught with crime where display of real jewellery could be positively dangerous. The paste Strass produced was soft enough to cut into any number of shapes which could then be set to follow

Foil-back green paste and colourless paste earrings c.1740. Rare and desirable, early paste was often mounted in gilt metal. Sandra Cronan

English mid- to late 18th century red foil-back and colourless paste flower cluster brooch. The combination of colours is rare and such a design would fetch a high sum today. Diana Foley

A late 18th/early 19th century opaline paste, colourless paste and silver sunburst brooch and double cluster brooch. The milky appearance is caused by separation of various oxides in the cooling process while the opalescent effect is obtained by setting over rose-colour tinfoil. Pat Novissimo

Two good examples of 'Queen Anne' paste in aquamarine blue and ruby red colours. Note the characteristic size differential between the two principal pastes in each brooch. Pat Novissimo

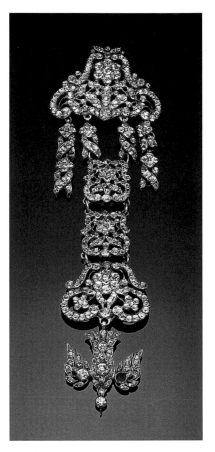

Fine English colourless paste and silver brooch with 'Saint Esprit' dove suspension. This elegant jewel extends to a total length of 7in. (17.78cm). Woolley & Wallis

the contours of the mount. In this way cushion, round and drop-shaped pastes were snugly set in silver or silver gilt which fully enclosed the back of the setting. In common with much 18th century jewellery, the individual pastes were backed with tinfoil to intensify brilliance and sometimes the front of the piece was decorated with strips of gold or little gold beads to add a touch of glitter.

French paste conformed to the same patterns fashionable in diamond jewellery such as sévigné bows, girandole drops, feathers, flower sprays and butterflies. English paste, however, veered towards the simple and altogether less elaborate. A common 18th century theme for brooches in diamonds or paste was the six-petal flower cluster, while Maltese crosses, curling plumes and uncomplicated leaf shapes are often encountered today. Late 18th century rings of both French and English origin followed the

English late 18th century colourless paste Maltese cross brooch.

Late 19th century colourless 'French' paste earrings and a necklace of colourless paste with imitation 'pearl' beads, c.1885. Good quality paste was made to imitate diamond jewellery of exactly the same design; the necklace would be convertible into a tiara. Private Collection

(Left) A group of late 19th century and early 20th century French paste bracelets, pendants and brooches. Usually mounted in silver, much of this material was unexceptional and individual pastes are often missing.

classical ideal such as large octagonal or marquise-shaped plaques enamelled in royal blue within paste borders while earrings were somewhat curiously set with two large but unmatched pastes in plain mounts with rather thick hook fittings on the back. Possibly the most wearable design for English mid- to late 18th century paste jewellery was the collet necklace, in which a series of graduated cushion-shaped sections mounted in dome-back gilt metal were each set with a fully faceted foiled paste. These were usually in standard colours meant to imitate real gems such as 'emerald' green or 'ruby' red but one particular variety stood out. Known as 'opaline', this pinkish-blue material was used extensively in necklaces, earrings, buttons and brooches where its soft rose colour foil was the ideal accompaniment for sparkling colourless paste.

Generally speaking, 19th century paste lacks the beauty, finish and 'density' of the 18th century variety. Necklaces, brooches and pendants could often appear rather cheap and flashy, unsurprising when one considers that the paste was uniform in shape, size and cut where a large number were set together to look like diamonds. The biggest development was the setting – or rather lack of it, since 19th century paste was left exposed at the back for all the available light to pass through. This did away with the need for foiling and – another development – gold began to be used rather more liberally.

19th century paste brooches, diadems, tiaras and necklaces copied their diamond counterparts faithfully. Heavier collet settings gradually gave way to lighter, thinner 'millegrain' settings and after 1840 the individual pastes were often 'silvered' to achieve a permanent glitter. As the century progressed, paste jewellery became increasingly versatile and plentiful

A group of Vauxhall glass brooches, pins and earrings. Unusual colours, particularly green and blue, are highly collectable today.   Pat Novissimo

with large numbers of cheap and pretty pendants manufactured in silver, brooches in an enormous range of designs including flowers, birds, animals, insects and reptiles and cluster necklaces and hair combs described generally as 'French paste'. Much of this kind of jewellery is, frankly, extremely cheap and cheerful and can easily deteriorate with careless handling.

Early 20th century paste was elegant and pretty, particularly pendants and brooches of 'Belle Époque' design which could sometimes mimic diamonds extremely well. By the 1930s paste double clips in highly polished 'chrome-like' mounts or geometric bracelets and necklaces copied expensive gems and exhibited the best of costume jewellery design, particularly pieces of French manufacture set with

well-cut 'ruby-red' or 'sapphire-blue' paste which combined visually bold materials with effortless style.

Vauxhall Glass

Known as 'mirror-back paste', this was a striking variety of paste fashionable in the 18th and early to mid-19th century. It originated at the Vauxhall Glass Works in London and usually took the form of highly reflective panels of glass set in floral clusters, stars or naturalistic designs which were invariably mounted in base metal as pendants, earrings, rings and diadems.

Further reading

Antique Paste Jewellery, M.D.S. Lewis (Boston Book and
    Art Publisher, USA)

CHAPTER 6

THE INDUSTRY OF DEATH: MEMENTO MORI AND MOURNING JEWELLERY

One of the more common varieties of antique jewellery one is likely to come across is a Victorian gilt metal and black enamel brooch inscribed 'In Memory Of.' In the centre a locket compartment will contain a plume of hair and the back of the mount will be engraved with the name of the deceased – long gone and sadly forgotten.

Today, the idea of placing the hair of a loved one into a brooch or ring would be seen as morbid, if not a little eccentric. Yet for over 350 years the fashion for wearing such jewellery remained consistently popular in a Britain which was both highly senti-mental and religiously devout. Milestone events such as the execution of Charles I, the death of Nelson and the premature loss of the Prince Consort – a catastrophe which plunged Queen Victoria into forty years of mourning – all played their part in fuelling public fascination in the 'Industry of Death.'

The 17th Century

During a period when disease, plague, war, infant mortality and malnutrition meant that life after forty was a comparative rarity, it was the custom for several identical gold rings to be bequeathed to principal mourners as a keepsake of the deceased. The more influential or celebrated the individual, the greater the number of rings which would be made and distributed. Thus when Charles I was executed in 1649 there was a massive demand amongst Royalist sympathisers for a memento and literally hundreds of gold and silver slides, pendants and rings were produced containing a portrait of the King, usually set under a cover of rock crystal.

The inevitability of death was summed up in the grim expression 'Remember that you must die', better known in its Latin translation, *Memento Mori*. 17th century memento mori jewels can be macabre and rather gruesome. A typical gold slide – worn on a black velvet ribbon – would contain a bed of human hair upon which rested a miniature coffin or a recumbent skeleton enamelled in white and black together with various symbols of mortality such as an hourglass or gravedigger's shovel. The back of these slides might be engraved with a simple monogram or date of death. It was not unknown to insert a piece of human skin into these extraordinary little lockets; clearly these are jewels for the purist. Stuart mourning rings also conformed to this stark

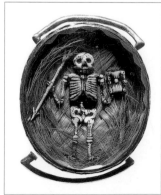

(Far left) Charles I Memento Mori *miniature c.1650. After the king's execution in 1649, gold slides containing his portrait and perhaps a lock of hair were distributed to Royalist sympathisers.*

(Left) Gold and rock crystal slide containing an enamelled skeleton on bed of woven hair c.1683. Not everyone's cup of tea but clearly resonant with the grim mortality of the time. Museum of London

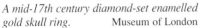

A mid-17th century diamond-set enamelled gold skull ring. Museum of London

(Above right) White enamel and gold memorial band ring c.1740. The skeleton extends around the entire hoop. White enamel meant that the deceased was unmarried.
Museum of London

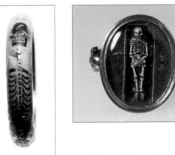

Gold ring with locket bezel containing a miniature enamel skeleton with scythe and hourglass motifs c.1720. This particularly good example is flanked by a miniature gold skull on each shoulder. Museum of London

ideal with enamelled death's head bezels set with diamonds in the eyes with crossed bones behind on a hoop fashioned in the design of an elongated skeleton.

The 18th Century

As time wore on, the stark symbolism of early memento mori jewels was gradually superseded by a gentler, altogether prettier range of mourning jewellery culminating at the end of the century in hopeless sentimentality.

Early 18th century rings were still enamelled in black and white with little crystal bezels, but pendants and slides began to be set with diamonds or gems such as garnets or rubies in heart-shaped frames. The use of white enamel after the 1750s inferred that the deceased was unmarried whilst the appearance of a coiled serpent with its tail gripped in its jaws suggested eternal love. Mid- to late 18th century mourning rings were typically designed as a

scrollwork band in which the name, date of birth and date of death of the individual would be highlighted in gold capitals on an enamelled field.

By the end of the century, mourning jewels – particularly brooches and pendants – became strongly romanticised. The frames were of simple, plain form and neo-classical in shape, usually octagonal, navette (pointed at both finials) or oval. Sorrowful rather than savage, these lockets contained little pictures under glass painted to depict distraught ladies prostrate by a plinth with a funerary urn and bearing the message 'Not Lost But Gone Before' or 'Asleep With Jesus'. A weeping willow tree picked out in hair would form the background and the miniature might be decorated with tiny seed glass pearls suggesting tears. Superior examples were bordered by enamel, sometimes with diamond highlights, whilst fine quality rings contained a classical urn studded with numerous diamonds on a bed of hair.

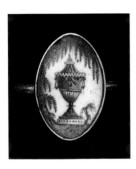

(Left) Late 18th century neo-classical funerary urn ring with characteristic 'weeping willow' decoration. English c.1785.

(Right) Late 18th century 'sentimental' hair jewellery. Surprisingly common today, the design of these jewels is strongly neo-classical.

 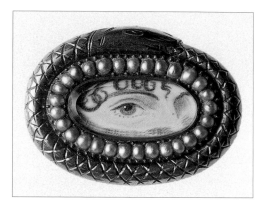 

(Above left) Late 18th century 'Sentimental' memorial slide. Finely painted in sepia brown, the foreground is picked out in hair. The row of little holes punched into the fittings at each end suggest this was mounted as a clasp on a multi-row seed pearl bracelet.

(Above centre) Late 18th/early 19th century gold brooch with painted eye miniature. 'Tear' jewellery is extremely collectable because of the limitless variations on a single theme. Note the coiled serpent surround symbolising eternity.

Museum of London

(Above right) Early Victorian gold lyre brooch woven with hair in the frame, c.1840.

Another curious manifestation of the time was the 'Tear' jewel in which a small gold slide or brooch would be painted on ivory with the miniature of a single eye weeping a solitary tear; charming and highly collectable.

The 19th Century
By the early 1800s mourning rings took the form of a broad gold band with hoops of black or white enamel bearing an inscription, while the romantic influence led to the appearance of gold locket rings set with clusters of half pearls symbolising tears, jet or French jet (faceted black glass). The enormous popularity of mourning jewellery in the 19th century led to the manufacture of literally hundreds of thousands of items so any example with the hair (and rock solid

Early Victorian gold earrings mounted with finely woven balls of hair, c.1840.

provenance) of a prominent figure would be considered highly collectable today. Monarchs (such as George III or George IV), war heroes (particularly Nelson, Wellington or Napoleon), politicians, actors and authors will fetch a considerable premium in price, although condition is usually a critical factor.

Much of the mourning jewellery made during Queen Victoria's reign was so romanticised as to barely hint at its true meaning. Gone were the morbid icons of death to be replaced by pretty plumes of hair tied with gold wire in borders of half pearls and frames of rococo gold. More recognisable brooches were poorly constructed from gilt metal and enamelled in jet black. Easy to damage and uncommercial, most Victorian mourning brooches are both cheap and easily available today.

In the 1840s and 1850s a fashion developed in which hair was finely woven into plaited ropes and delicate openwork 'balls' suitable for earrings or 'tubes' for brooches. Hair is surprisingly robust and it is still possible to come across perfect jewellery composed entirely of hair mounted in gold fittings. Unfortunately, unscrupulous jewellers resorted to the use of horsehair which was both plentiful and easy to work. Horsehair jewellery is a decorative material

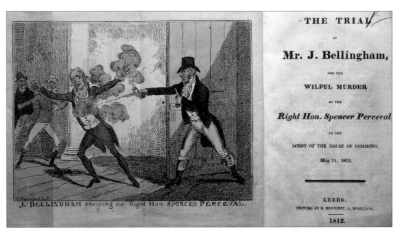

A pair of enamelled gold bands dedicated to Spencer Perceval, assassinated on 11 May, 1812.

A coloured engraving by George Cruikshank describing the heinous deed. Spencer Perceval was Prime Minister at the time of his murder. The combination of political memorabilia, a violent end and the fine condition of the rings (left) indicate a value of several thousand pounds today.

An onyx and gold memorial brooch in a gold and black enamel Grecian key pattern frame.

The back of the same brooch is inscribed and dated 1876.

distinct from the human variety and is occasionally found today in elaborate necklaces and bracelets dyed off-white or coral red.

The prime material which we most closely associate with mourning jewellery is, of course, jet. After the death of the Prince Consort in 1861, the jet industry located at Whitby on the North Yorkshire coast produced thousands of carved brooches, necklaces, bracelets and crosses supplied by scores of little shops which sprang up to cater for the public demand. The range of products was extraordinarily diverse and on the whole highly proficient. Today there are still excellent specialist jet shops in Whitby. Prices, however, reflect the quality and skill of the craftsmen, so early original pieces can fetch several hundred pounds for a good necklace or cameo brooch.

After the death of Victoria there was a conscious desire to embrace a lighter, more frivolous lifestyle so clearly absent for forty years and the very British passion for mourning jewellery evaporated almost overnight. It is difficult to imagine it ever being revived.

Further reading

Antique and 20th Century Jewellery, Vivienne Becker (NAG Press)

Jewellery in Britain 1066-1837, Diana Scarisbrick (Michael Russell Publishing Ltd.)

Jet Jewellery and Ornaments, Helen Muller (Shire Publications Ltd.)

French jet brooch of Bacchante, c.1870.
Courtesy of the Akiba Museum of Antique Jewellery, Japan

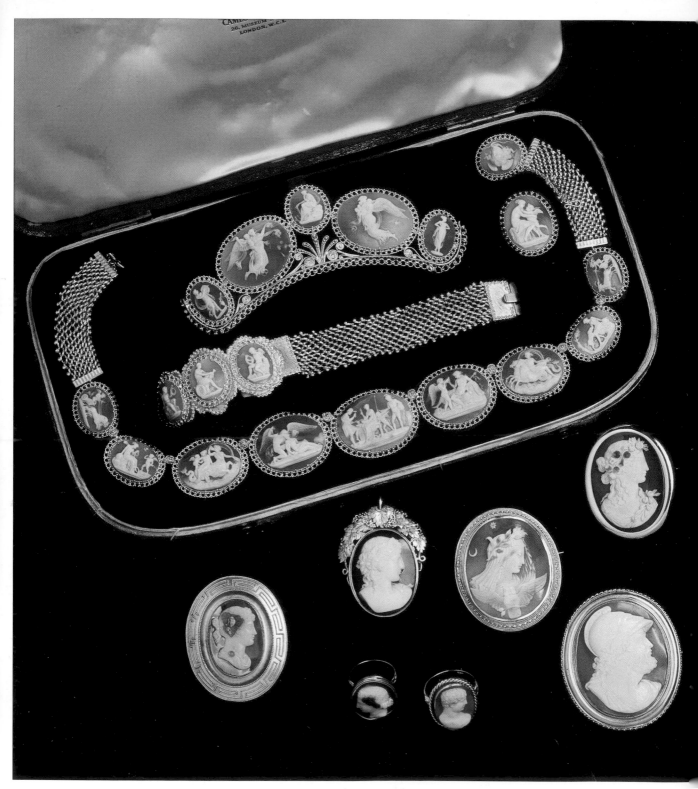

An early 19th century shell cameo and gold neo-classical parure in fitted 'Cameo Corner' case together with a range of 19th century hardstone and shell cameo brooches and rings.

Private Collection/Bridgeman Art Library

76

CHAPTER 7

CAMEOS AND INTAGLIOS

Imust say that I feel a particularly close affinity with this subject since I started my career at an antique jewellery shop near the British Museum in Bloomsbury, London called Cameo Corner. First, a definition of the two media:

A cameo is a carving in which the design stands out in relief from its background and an intaglio is a gem in which the design has been carved into the surface.

This is a technical description, but there is another important difference between cameos and intaglios: the former are visually striking and thus extremely wearable, whereas the latter are subtle, understated miniature works of art usually more of interest to the academic collector.

CAMEOS

The vast majority of cameos which appear on the market today are 19th century or later. Roman cameo rings are rare and occasionally turn up in specialised auctions of antiquities and Renaissance cameos are exceedingly scarce, tricky to identify and often imperfect. 18th century cameos are more common but are easy to date incorrectly. Their settings can assist in making an accurate judgment.

Condition is all when valuing cameos. They were meant to be worn and shell, the most common material we see today, is a soft organic material which routinely fractures, breaks or simply wears smooth with regular use so the surface features become indistinct. A fine unworn cameo with a lovely female head in profile in an undamaged gold frame will thus command a considerable premium, whilst a tired, split old cameo in a frame smothered in lead repairs can be bought very cheaply.

Shell Cameos

Although shell cameo carving is found in 16th century jewellery, nearly all shell cameos mounted in jewellery are 19th century or later. The industry was first developed in Sicily, then Naples, and Italian craftsmen worked in France and England in the 1850s

Italian shell cameo necklace depicting classical female deities in gold rope pattern frames c.1880. The swag-like connecting chains are called 'en esclavage'.
Woolley & Wallis

77

(Left) Italian 19th century shell cameo and gold brooch c.1865. The subject matter is finely carved and very commercial. S.J. Phillips

(Right) A standard Italian shell cameo brooch c.1870 carved to depict 'Night and Day.' Woolley & Wallis

and 1860s. Most shell cameos are caramel brown and white and are cut from a large helmet-shaped natural seashell called *Cassis tuberosa*. Pink shell cameos were taken from the queen conch shell and tend to be confused with coral. Sometimes these large and imposing seashells were themselves carved to display a mythological scene or classical group and were placed in shop windows for display purposes.

Hardstone Cameos

The great advantage of hardstone is that it can be carved in far greater detail than shell (which is much softer) and, furthermore, the contrasting background colour will take a near mirror-like polish. Hardstone cameos are somewhat heavy, creating a tendency for brooches to fall forward when pinned on an outfit. They are almost always more expensive than shell.

Classical pink and white agate brooch in a gold cannetille frame c.1835-45. Bentley & Skinner

Fine bejewelled black and white onyx cameo habillé of a Nubian princess in matching ruby and diamond frame c.1880. Hancocks

Carved malachite cameo of a classical deity in a black enamel frame set with emeralds c.1840-50. S.J. Phillips

Superb mid-19th century Italian gold architectural necklace mounted with various onyx and sardonyx classical cameos.
S.J. Phillips

The principal varieties are:

Sardonyx: rust-brown or pinkish-brown background with white or cream carving.

Onyx: jet black background (sometimes stained) with white carving.

Agate: usually a dove-grey background with white carving.

Malachite and Lapis Lazuli: used in late 18th and early 19th century parures and often carved with neo-classical scenes.

19th century lava cameo pendant. Such 'Vesuvian' laval cameos appeared in a range of colours and subjects. Clearly made for the tourist market, the settings were usually gilt metal or low carat gold and rather crude.

Sylvie Spectrum

An Italian coral cameo brooch in an enamelled gold frame together with a pale pink and white conch shell cameo brooch. Pink shell is often confused with coral; it was a popular medium used extensively in inexpensive dress rings and tiepins at the end of the 19th century. RBR Group at Grays

Neo-classical blue jasperware plaque mounted as a clasp in a polished steel and cut steel frame c.1800.

RBR Group of Grays

Precious and Semi-Precious Gem Cameos

Rare and very expensive, rubies, sapphires and emeralds have been fashioned into cameos since ancient times. Usually small and of simple design due to their ungiving hardness, one is most likely to find a rare, precious gem cameo in a Roman ring and very occasionally in a simple 18th century gold setting. Two less valuable but colourful gems which appear in late 19th century brooches are golden citrine and purple amethyst. The greater size of these stones meant that carvings were usually intricate in detail with profiles including classical heads and ladies in Tudor costume. Another gem which is sometimes found in turn of the century rings and brooches was opal, carved with a range of unusual subjects such as Red Indian chiefs and exotic animals in which the natural colours and contours of the stone added to the effectiveness of the carving.

Lava Cameos

Popular with travellers on the Grand Tour, volcanic lava from Mount Vesuvius ranged in colour from chalk white through beige, terracotta, pale grey to dark grey and black. Subjects included famous philosophers, statesmen and historical figures such as Leonardo da Vinci and Shakespeare. Usually simply set in low-grade gold mounts as brooches, bracelets or complete parures.

Other Organic Materials

These included coral, extensively used in the 18th and 19th centuries, ivory, where quite large brooches were set in very basic frames, and jet, a very English phenomenon in which flower studies were just as popular as the standard classical head in profile.

Imitation Materials

An imitation cameo usually suggests a cheap copy. Certainly, some of the plastic and composition cameos produced in the 1930s-1950s are pretty basic, but 19th century glass cameos can be very effective. These were usually deep purple or blue, imposing in size and portrayed the head of Bacchante in profile. The frames, as expected, are in base metal.

Josiah Wedgwood produced blue and white jasper stoneware in the 18th century which can be mistaken for cameos. Most subjects were neo-classical and the frames were usually metal or cut steel.

Finally, some early twentieth century costume cameos are composition doublets, in which the bust has been glued to the background.

Subjects and Their Settings

Considering their age, many medieval and later cameos are remarkably accomplished although extremely scarce today. 16th and 17th century cameos do appear occasionally at auctions of early rings and antiquities. The carvings are shallow and sometimes irregular in shape while fine quality examples may be set in bright yellow gold frames embellished with colourful enamel, diamonds and pearls.

The two guiding themes of 18th and 19th century cameo cutting were classicism and romanticism. From the mid-18th century to the early 19th century, neo-classical cameos represented the very finest execution of detail and realism. Subjects were noble and powerful including mythological deities, Greek and Roman philosophers and emperors, prominent statesmen and figures from the Church, nobility and military. The frames were usually simple rims of gold known as 'Roman' seal settings. Sometimes

these individual cameos were joined together as necklaces or bracelets by three or four tiers of fine gold chains called *en esclavage.*

Early 19th century cameos often depicted complete groups of mythological figures and animals with little cherubs known as *putti* in attendance. Carved in hardstone, shell or occasionally malachite, the settings gradually became more elaborate so by the 1830s and 1840s many cameos were framed in intricate gold filigree surrounds known as *cannetille* work.

The early Victorian era heralded an age of romanticism. Cool classicism gave way to a softer, less austere definition of cameo carving in which the female form predominated (Bacchante, Minerva, and Medusa were hugely popular). This diversification led to all sorts of subjects appearing on cameo brooches; naturalism and realism competed with scenes from the Bible, ladies in Tudor costumes, figures standing in a rustic landscape and profiles of Victorian gentlemen on the Grand Tour immortalised by Italian carvers such as Tommaso and Luigi Saulini.

From the 1860s to the 1880s Italian craftsmen mounted bold hardstone cameos in fine yellow gold frames decorated with twisted wirework and shotwork motifs. Subject matter was again strongly classical, verging on the heroic. Popular mythological deities – Apollo, Mars, Diana and Mercury –

(Left) 16th century blue and white agate cameo exhibiting characteristic Renaissance realism. S.J. Phillips

(Right) A charming late 18th century cameo ring of two lovebirds in a diamond frame signed in Greek characters by Giovanni Pichler (1734-1791).

Archaeological gold revival parure together with two unmounted hardstone cameos, c.1865. Although unsigned, the finely worked floral detail in the frames is characteristic of Castellani. The colour and subject matter of the unmounted cameo depicting Dante at centre left makes this particular example rather unsaleable.

Black and white onyx cameo brooch/pendant with matching earrings. Italian c.1865. Woolley & Wallis

were carved in high relief from onyx, sardonyx and pale grey agate.

By the end of the century the fashion and passion for cameos dwindled. 20th century cameos, sometimes set in nine carat gold or silver with marcasite highlights, lack the subtlety and detail of earlier examples and mass-production in the modern era has resulted in some very crude, repetitive and charmless carvings being sold by high street jewellers.

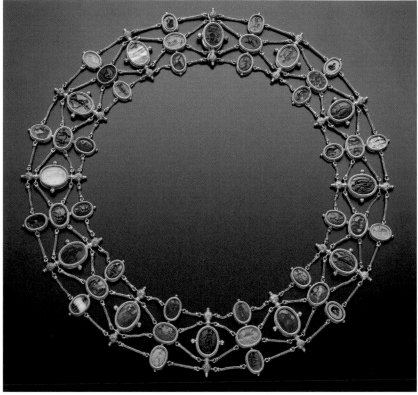

*Ancient intaglios in their orig-
inal gold settings and an intaglio
hardstone seal set in a late
18th century gold 'swivelling'
bezel (centre). Swivel settings
were particularly favoured by
gem engravers such as Marchant
and Pichler.*

*Splendid archaeological gold collar mounted with an assortment of classical intaglios.
The combination of both ancient and contemporary hardstones was a common feature of
18th century neo-classical and 19th century Revivalist jewellery.* S.J. Phillips

INTAGLIOS

These perfect little works of art represent some of the
very oldest examples of stone cutting and gem
embellishment existing today. They are difficult to wear
individually although in the 18th century it was
fashionable to mount fine examples by prominent gem
engravers as finger rings in gold 'Roman style' seal
settings. Regency necklaces composed of twenty or
more genuine Roman intaglios in several different
colours of hardstone were invariably seal set in gold,
whilst classical revival goldsmiths such as Castellani
used ancient intaglios in some of his architectural jewels.

There were several important gem engravers
active in the 18th century whose work is highly
collectable today. Nathaniel Marchant (1739-1816)
worked in Rome as a portrait engraver. Edward
Burch (1730-1814) exhibited at the Royal Academy
and specialised in historical profiles, while Giovanni
Pichler (1734-1791) and his half-brother Luigi
(1773-1854) specialised in superb engravings of
classical heads and groups in a range of different
hardstones. Prince Stanislaw Poniatowski (1754-
1833) amassed a large collection of cornelian
intaglios with faked signatures while James Tassie
(1735-1799), a Scotsman, produced large numbers
of imitation gems in glass which regularly appear in
sizeable numbers on the market today.

Further reading

*The Art of the Jeweller: A Catalogue of the Hull Grundy Gift
to the British Museum* (British Museum Publications Ltd.)
Engraved Gems, John Boardman (Thames & Hudson)

CHAPTER 8
MOSAICS

Colourful, evocative and intricate, mosaics provided some of the most expressive and proficient examples of the craftsman's skill in which the smallest possible materials were amalgamated to create a work of art in miniature.

Inspired by the frescoes, ceilings and floors of ancient Roman interiors, mosaics used in jewellery depicted the sort of subjects which the expanding numbers of visitors to Italy most admired: historic buildings like the Colosseum and Pantheon, architectural sites such as St Peter's, Rome, as well as a wide variety of classical and romantic symbols – cherubs, domestic and wild animals, evocative ruins, colourful flower studies and swooping birds.

Mosaics were not only confined to small scale plaques set into brooches or necklaces. Some of the most virtuosi examples of the craft were reserved for large scale objets d'art such as wall plaques and table tops in which the sheer quantity of tiny individual pieces of coloured glass used to fill such a large surface area is, frankly, extremely difficult to comprehend.

There were two principal varieties of mosaics differentiated by the name of the city from which they originated.

Roman Mosaics

In recent years, the term 'Roman mosaic' has been superseded by the rather less inspiring description 'micromosaic' to avoid any possible 'historic' confusion. Roman mosaic can trace its roots back to the Renaissance when a Vatican workshop was established in the late 16th century. By the 18th century large numbers of tourists visiting Rome on the Grand Tour triggered widespread popular interest in the medium leading to inevitable commercial exploitation.

Roman mosaics are decorative plaques, usually oval or rectangular, in which thousands of tiny pieces of coloured glass or stone were carefully selected, positioned and cemented together to create a recognisable picture. These fragments were known as *tesserae* and were usually made by cutting up rods of glass which had been stretched in order that hundreds of subtle shades of colour could be introduced into the material itself. The technique was not entirely dissimilar from *millefiore* in which clusters of coloured glass were grouped like so many sticks of rock, sliced up and mounted together in bead necklaces and paperweights. The sheer range of colour means that tesserae which fall out of antique mosaic jewels are almost impossible to replicate – one very good reason why perfect pieces are significantly more expensive than damaged ones.

Early Roman mosaics – those dating from the 18th and early 19th century – are superior (and dearer) than 19th century examples because the size of the individual fragments of tesserae are that much smaller. Early mosaics are much more subtle and better defined, often appearing like miniature oil

Micromosaic and gold brooch depicting the Capitoline Doves, c.1860. Commonly known as 'Pliny's Doves', a subject immortalised by Pliny the Elder in his History of Art, *this large and colourful plaque exhibits the deft skill and painstaking craft necessary in setting line upon line of minute glass fragments to form a recognisable picture.*

Italian neo-classical micromosaic bracelet and earrings depicting popular architectural ruins with their original fitted case, c.1825-30.
Bonhams, London/Bridgeman Art Library

(Above) Early 19th century Roman mosaic landscape full of detail, colour and movement. Generally speaking, these older mosaics were composed of very small tesserae and were thus considerably smoother and finer than later examples which often betray a rough and rather coarse finish. Woolley & Wallis

(Right) Italian micromosaic and gold necklace and a similarly set cross c.1860-1870. Colourful and intricate in their execution, 'Roman' mosaic subjects favoured sentimental themes such as birds and cherubs while architectural symbolism was always in demand. (See Frontispiece.) S.J. Phillips

paintings, smooth to the touch and so cleverly set that the cement between each fragment is barely visible. 19th century mosaics, on the other hand, are coarser, cruder, uneven to the touch and somewhat two-dimensional in appearance.

Early mosaics were strongly neo-classical in theme. Landscapes with rivers and waterfalls, pastoral and hunting scenes and domestic animals (particularly dogs) were typical of the period, along with romantic doves, cherubs and assorted symbols of sentiment. These mosaics were simply set in plain gold rims or joined together by tiers of fine gold chains as necklaces or pairs of bracelets. In the 1830s and 1840s mosaics were set in elaborate gold cannetille frames combining neo-classical and romantic themes. The colour of the background tesserae was usually white and it was popular to encircle the individual designs within borders and backs of blue or red glass. Sometimes bright gold tesserae were introduced to reinforce the 'classical' impression.

By the 1860s and 1870s Egyptian Revivalism resulted in bright and colourful mosaics depicting

Superb archaeological gold and micromosaic bracelet by Castellani c.1860. S.J. Phillips

standard symbols with which tourists could easily identify – scarab beetles, the heads of Pharoahs, cobras and vultures. In yellow gold frames decorated with wire loops, twisted rope and soldered beads called shotwork, the word 'subtle' is less than appropriate; such Revivalist jewels would occasionally bear raised lettering with the words 'pax' or 'Roma' just in case one forgot from where the piece had originated.

Florentine Mosaics

Whilst Roman mosaics were invariably set with glass tesserae, the individual petals and leaves which formed the floral studies in Florentine mosaics were almost always colourful hardstones such as white chalcedony, red sard, sky blue turquoise, royal blue lapis lazuli, pink marble and mottled green malachite. The background used was dull black Belgian slate which was cut out and carefully filled with the appropriate piece of shaped hardstone in much the same way as a jigsaw puzzle. The effect of white and pastel colours against a jet black background was incredibly effective; lilies of the valley and sprays of forget-me-nots were powerfully portrayed in bright yellow gold frames enhanced, like

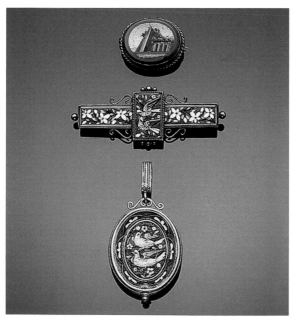

Group of micromosaic souvenir jewellery c.1880. The 'pyramid' brooch at the top is in a chipped blue glass surround; the frame of the 'birds' pendant is fashioned in silver gilt to keep costs as realistic as possible.
Author's collection

87

(Above) Florentine mosaic pendant, c.1870-80. This example is certainly colourful and effective but rather lacks the subtlety of the flower studies below. Woolley & Wallis

(Above centre) Micromosaic stick pin c.1880. By the end of the 19th century, mass production of mosaics resulted in a visible loss of quality. The subject, an iridescent beetle is, attractive but note the crude white tesserae. Private Collection

(Above right) Late 19th century Florentine mosaic stick pin. Note how badly cut the individual hardstone pieces are compared with earlier pietra dura examples. Private Collection

Roman mosaic, with rope pattern decoration. The technique of inlaying colourful hardstones into a contrasting background is known as *pietra dura* (literally 'hardstone') and can be seen in the wonderful collection of mosaics forming the Gilbert Collection on display at Somerset House in London.

Decorative Mosaics

Towards the end of the 19th century and the start of the 20th century, small and cheap pieces of souvenir jewellery and miniature accessories were set with colourful – and coarse – mosaic in low grade silver gilt or gilt metal mounts. These were surprisingly common but are still fairly effective, fashioned in designs ranging from novelty objects such as 'guitars' and 'bicycles' to prosaic button brooches and pretty little picture frames. A rather crude variety of Florentine mosaic made of shiny glass was also used in late 19th century costume jewellery, but this is difficult to confuse with the genuine material.

Further reading

The Gilbert Collection: Hardstones (Philip Wilson Publishers Ltd.)

Antique and 20th Century Jewellery, Vivienne Becker (NAG Press)

Florentine 'pietra dura' and gold bracelet c.1870 in which coloured marbles and hardstones are used to form delicate flower arrangements in a background of black Belgian slate. The mounts with accompanying wirework decoration are typical and note the batons in between each plaque, a feature of 19th century Italian 'Revivalist' jewellery.

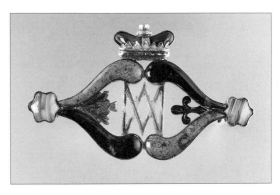

CHAPTER 9
JEWELLERY IN SCOTLAND

Whenever we think of 'Scottish jewellery', we automatically associate the term with those distinctive Victorian gold and silver brooches and bracelets mounted with citrines, rock crystals and a variety of colourful hardstone sections which fall under the catch-all definition of 'pebble jewels.'

As popular and collectable as this type of jewellery has become in recent years, it is also important to recognise the significance of Scotland in the history of decorative metalwork over the past five hundred years. Mary Queen of Scots was enormously influential in the manner in which ladies of nobility wore their jewellery, favouring pearls above all gems, mounted within gold pendants which were further embellished with colourful enamel, set with hardstone cameos or decorated with simple table-cut diamonds and polished gems. Rings – worn extensively throughout Scotland and England – took on a new significance after the execution of Charles I in 1649 when large numbers of Royalist mementoes were produced containing an enamelled portrait of the unfortunate king. In Scotland sympathisers of the Jacobite cause wore similar miniatures depicting Prince Charles Edward Stuart, better known as Bonnie Prince Charlie. Simple ring brooches of flattened form made from gold, silver and base metal – as functional as they were decorative – were used to fasten the material of coarse plaid worn by women during the 17th and 18th century. Ring brooches can still be picked up quite cheaply and sometimes exhibit beautiful engraving, complex in its intricacy. Another popular Scottish brooch, the luckenbooth, was worn as a good luck token offering protection against the 'evil eye'. Usually made from silver or brass, designs were based on the heart and could be extremely

(Above) Good quality Scottish vari-colour agate brooch with crown surmount and Queen Mary monogram to the centre. Note the combined French and Scottish fleur-de-lis and thistle motifs. Ginny Redington Dawes

(Left) Group of three silver or gold luckenbooth brooches. The example at the bottom is sometimes referred to as a witch's heart. Brian and Lynn Holmes

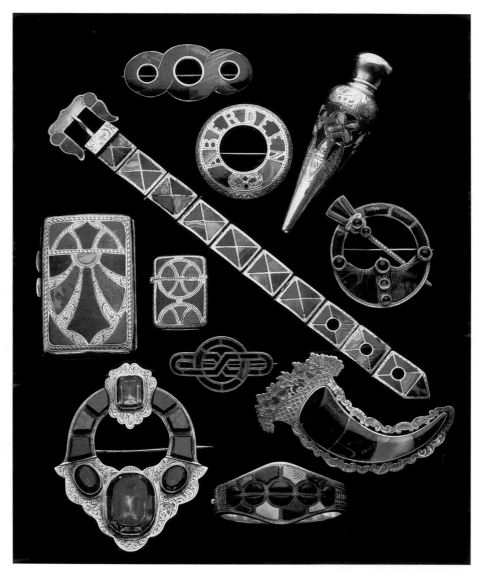

Scottish group including a fine silver plaid brooch at bottom left mounted with foil-back amethyst and 'Cairngorm' citrine. Note the discoloration caused by water damage.

simple or highly elaborate. Some luckenbooths contained a monogram of two entwined hearts shaped like the letter 'M' which were known as Queen Mary brooches.

Queen Victoria's tremendous affection for Scotland is well known. In 1848 she purchased Balmoral Castle and in those happier days before the untimely death of Prince Albert in 1861 the Royal children customarily wore tartan dress, whilst at the Great Exhibition Ball of 1851 all the guests were expected to wear Scottish dress adorned with jewelled accessories such as brooches, dirks and buckles. This high romanticised idealism was further reinforced by Sir Walter Scott who wrote passionately about the sweeping grandeur of the hills and valleys, so articulating an emotional fascination with Scotland which, even today, has barely diminished.

By the 1850s Scotland's soaring popularity resulted in large numbers of people visiting the country, all clamouring for a souvenir of their holiday. A pretty hardstone brooch, curio or accessory served this purpose admirably. Scottish hardstone or 'pebble'

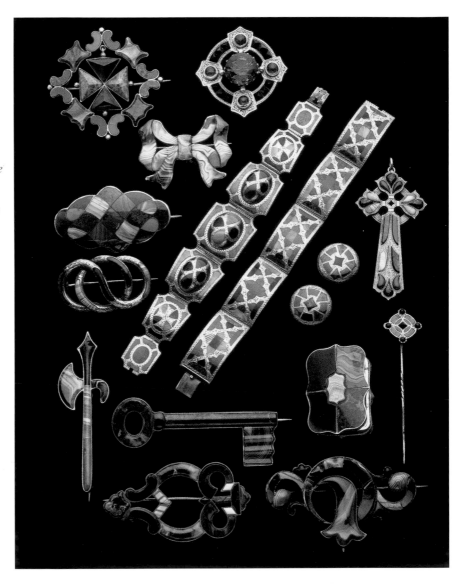

Scottish jewellery in gold and silver mounts. Condition is a critical issue since missing hardstones are extremely difficult and costly to replace. Novelties such as keys and axes or accessories such as the vinaigrette at lower right are rare and desirable today.

jewellery was largely inspired by the established designs of centuries old Celtic and folk jewellery. Probably the best example was the silver plaid brooch which was used to secure the tartan at the shoulder. These large ring-shaped brooches were often set to the centre with an imposing golden brown citrine called, appropriately enough, a cairngorm. In other examples the cairngorm would be substituted by a very pale lemon yellow citrine, a colourless rock crystal or even golden glass. It was also common to leave the centre aperture entirely vacant. The broad silver frames

would then be mounted with a series of vari-coloured hardstone panels, individually cut and shaped to fit the contours of the hoop-shaped surround. The colour of these hardstones were, in themselves, highly suggestive of the wild cragginess of the Scottish countryside, blending the rich browns, yellows, greys and russet shades of heath and heather, mountain and stream. Thus, a typical Scottish silver brooch would be composed of a combination of orangy-brown cornelian, subtle grey banded agate, deep green bloodstone with its characteristic flecks of red, mottled jasper with

Unusual vari-colour agate coiled serpent bangle c.1860.
Ginny Redington Dawes

Scottish novelty souvenirs. Although inexpensive when first manufactured, such easily recognisable mementoes would fetch good prices today. Ginny Redington Dawes

curious marbling of red, mustard and black, and onyx with distinctive bands of black and white.

Cutting these stones was often difficult and many were sent to Idar Oberstein in Germany for finishing and polishing. These thin stone slices would then be set into plain or engraved silver mounts, often with a black tar-like shellac material behind to strengthen the colours when seen from the front. Apart from citrine and rock crystal, the other crystalline material in

frequent use was amethyst, a particularly appropriate gemstone when carved into the shape of thistles.

Plaid brooches and thistles were just two examples of a broad range of Scottish themes, including miniature dirks with tiny removable daggers slotted in the front, rapiers with polished hardstone shafts, hearts, knots, buckles, straps, shields and anchors. The use of hardstones was not purely confined to jewellery; indeed a whole spectrum of practical small accessories was also produced including vesta boxes, vinaigrettes and sovereign cases.

By 1870 over one thousand people were directly or indirectly employed in Edinburgh alone in the pebble industry and smaller communities thrived in Aberdeen, Glasgow and even as far south as Birmingham. The Aberdeen firm of Rettie & Co was particularly associated with a locally extracted pink and grey granite which proved an effective combination when set in geometric brooches and bracelets. Not all the hardstones were indigenous to Scotland, however. Malachite, frequently carved into the shape of ivy leaves, was actually imported from the frozen wastes of Siberia, via Germany.

Although the majority of Scottish pebble jewellery was mounted in silver, some extremely fine pieces were also fashioned in gold. Bracelets, for example,

Group of Scottish silver, agate, granite, malachite and hardstone earrings c.1860. Ginny Redington Dawes

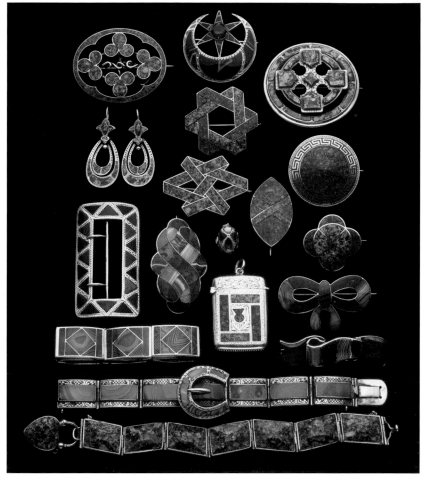

Group of Scottish hardstone and silver 'pebble' jewels and accessories. The combination of pink and grey granite was a speciality of Rettie & Co, a firm based in Aberdeen which cut and polished material extracted from local quarries.

were either composed of hinged sections decorated with flat polished hardstone panels in 'marquetry' formation or in three-dimensional 'barrels' with engraved gold cap fittings.

Scotland was also an important location for the Arts and Crafts movement at the end of the 19th century, standing out for the incredible wealth of creative talent which seemed to gravitate to the Glasgow School of Art. Here innovative craftsmen and women formed close working (and personal) relationships producing a wonderful range of decorative arts both rich in symbolism and proficient in technical application. Probably the best known of all these exponents was Charles Rennie Mackintosh (1869-1929) who pioneered groundbreaking organic forms in furniture and interiors.

Among many designer jewellers, three women made a particular impact: Jessie M. King (1873-1949) was a somewhat eccentric illustrator who also made silk fabrics for Liberty & Co and designed naturalistic gold jewellery for the London store; Mary Thew (1869-1929) was a metalworker who used abalone shell in interesting Celtic brooches whilst Phoebe Anna Traquair (1852-1936) was probably the most versatile and celebrated of all the Glasgow School goldsmiths producing beautiful, glowing enamelled gold necklaces and pendants heavily influenced by the work of the Pre-Raphaelite movement.

Further reading

Victorian Jewelry: Unexplored Treasures, Ginny Redington Dawes and Corinne Davidov (Abbeville Press Publishers)

The Art of Jewellery in Scotland, edited by R.K. Marshall and G.R. Dalgleish (Scottish National Portrait Gallery)

A group of Victorian, Edwardian and later insect, reptile and assorted 'wildlife' brooches illustrating the range of designs available to collectors. The snail with conchoidal diamond shell is an interesting rarity, and note the rather lifelike tiger's eye cabochons in the pair of bumblebees.

CHAPTER 10
JEWELLED FLORA AND FAUNA

Flowers, from the basic trefoil of three petals to massive bouquets worn as corsage ornaments by the aristocracy, have underpinned jewellery design since the 17th century. Early floral sprays were usually enamelled in several colours since gemstone cutting, particularly diamond, was still fairly rudimentary.

As time progressed designs became increasingly lavish, especially when gold replaced silver as the standard metal. 18th century diamond brooches and aigrette sprays could be extremely flamboyant, setting hundreds of diamonds in pavé formation with superb coloured gems such as Burmese rubies and

(Above) English diamond flower brooch c.1850. This spray of wild rose is faithful to the genuine article as observed in the detail of the rosebuds. The principal flowerhead is mounted 'en tremblant' allowing the bloom to scintillate when worn.

(Left) Georgian flat-cut garnet flower spray brooch c.1800.

Indian emeralds highly prized for their exquisite colour and rarity. Many jewelled bouquets were embellished with tied bows around the stems allowing individual craftsmen to show off their skill by deftly weaving trails of ribbon within their framework. English late 18th century diamond brooches often conformed to a simple and highly effective design in which six uniform size petals were fully enclosed in silver and pavé-set with clusters of 'old-mine' diamonds of pure quality surrounding a larger stone to the centre. Tasteful, practical and perfectly wearable today, Georgian diamond flowers attract strong competition when they appear at auction.

A particularly charming example of 18th century naturalistic jewellery was the *giardinetti* ring or brooch. These 'little gardens' were set with a cluster of rose diamonds, emeralds, rubies and occasionally sapphires in floral compositions in which the principal gem sometimes formed a stylised vase. Care should be taken since many cheap and inferior modern copies regularly turn up on the market; the later examples are often badly set with modern cut stones.

Floral jewellery of the early 19th century was delicate and feminine in inspiration. Brooches, earrings and necklaces placed great emphasis on gold work in which the settings were finely textured,

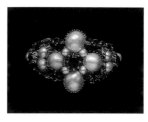

(Above) Victorian half pearl, ruby and gold quatrefoil cluster ring c.1845. These pretty little rings usually contained a locket compartment at the back of the bezel for a tiny lock of hair. Woolley & Wallis

(Above right) Fine example of a Georgian ruby and diamond Giardinetti or 'little garden' ring. Sandra Cronan

(Below) A set of six matching French gold, royal blue enamel and seed pearl 'lace pins' c.1840. Note the subtle differences between each little floral study. Mrs Vicky Waller

realistically engraved to represent leaves, embellished with wirework tendrils or complicated granulation and cannetille scrolls. There was far greater use of colourful semi-precious stones such as amethyst, aquamarine, topaz and turquoise which were ideal companions for naturalistic and floral designs. Turquoise in particular was liberally used in flower jewellery of the 1830s and 1840s because of its direct association with forget-me-not. The bright blue gem was thus the perfect vehicle for expressing affection and sentiment captured in charming dove brooches bearing messages of love in their beaks, ears of corn and woodland sprays.

Another gem which was ideally suited to the naturalistic passion was coral. A speciality of Italy and particularly associated in England with Robert Phillips,

Unusual ruby and diamond pear brooch c.1850. A prime example of Victorian realism, the mount is embellished with two translucent green enamel leaves.

A group of Giuliano enamelled gold butterfly brooches c.1870. These delightfully realistic studies are exquisitely observed and represent some of the most charming examples of Carlo Giuliano's skill as an enameller.

Ghastly Victorian realism in the form of a humming bird head with solid gold beak and ruby cabochon eyes c.1870.

Victorian gold ring fashioned as two entwined snakes with gem-set heads c.1860. Snakes were a universally popular expression of eternal love or a powerful symbol of wisdom.

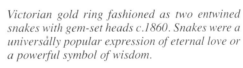

the celebrated London jeweller, coral was of sufficient hardness to carve into all manner of highly elaborate designs such as sprays of flowers with accompanying leaves and buds or 'woodland' themes such as trees and branches. Coral also takes a satisfyingly high polish and larger pieces were reserved for rather extraordinary and imaginative forms such as grotesques, satyrs, sea serpents and monsters which ingeniously conformed to the shape of the original material. Much of this type of

coral was a characteristic salmon pink colour, but white coral was also suitable for pretty flower brooches and necklaces carved into sprays of orange blossom or convolvulus with little rubies studded in their engraved gold mounts.

The 19th century fixation with nature extended to animals, birds, reptiles and insects. The snake was especially popular in the 1840s and 1850s and considerable numbers of necklaces, bracelets and

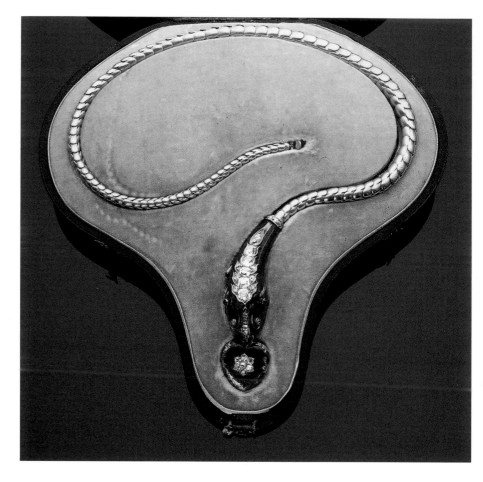

A fine early Victorian gold snake necklace with diamond encrusted royal blue enamelled head suspending a heart locket c.1845. Typically cobra-like, the value of this particular example is enhanced by its original fitted case. This design would easily be replicated as a coiled bangle or even a matching ring.

rings were produced in bright yellow gold, fully articulated to suggest the sinuous flow of the serpent's body with cobra-like heads set with diamonds and gems enamelled in royal blue, sky blue or even studded all the way round with scores of little cabochons of turquoise. Usually a heart-shaped pendant containing a lock of hair was suspended from the reptile's mouth and the eyes were set with ruby or garnet cabochons. Snakes represented 'love eternal' in Victorian England and were thus a potent symbol of sentiment as well as a highly effective design for fashion jewellery.

Victorian tiger claw stickpin 1890 and Victorian tiger tooth stickpin. Bengal tigers were shot with depressing frequency in the days of the Raj. These rather gruesome mementoes were mounted by Indian goldsmiths, sometimes into complete suites of necklace, earrings, bracelet and brooch. Private Collection

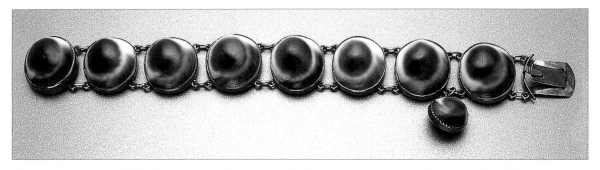

Operculum bracelet c.1850. These unusual Victorian curiosities were extracted from the shells of snail-like molluscs in which they formed a protective 'lid' or cover.

Another mid-Victorian curiosity was the *reverse crystal* where a domed piece of colourless rock crystal was carved from behind and painted with the image of an animal, bird, insect or flower. Designs were limitless and examples ranged from favourite domestic pets such as pug dogs, cats and even goldfish to wild animals of which lions, tigers and foxes were especially popular. The little paintings were often colourful and highly accomplished; bumble bees were so realistic that many people assume today that the insect is genuine, perpetually trapped beneath a magnifying dome of crystal. Mounted in gold with backplates of mother-of-pearl, reverse crystal is extremely collectable either in large-scale brooches or small-scale stickpins and cufflinks.

By the end of the 19th century 'scatter bugs' fashioned in gold and silver and set with diamonds and appropriately colourful gems were produced in an enormous range of designs from spiders, flies, bees and butterflies to reptiles, in particular frogs

Reverse crystal and gold bumble bee pendant c.1870. Hugely popular, these intricate painted miniatures encompassed a vast range of subjects from domestic pets to exotic Bengal tigers and decorative birds.

Reverse crystal stag pendant in a pearl-set gold frame c.1870.
S.H. Harris

Pair of reverse crystal fish and fishing fly cufflinks c.1890.
S.H. Harris

Opal and diamond dragonfly brooch with ruby eyes c.1900. A fine example of articulated turn of the century naturalism.

and salamanders.

These cleverly fashioned lizards were often set with diamonds and demantoids, the lovely and valuable green variety of commonplace red garnet in which the striking green colour aptly suggested the skin tone of the living creature.

Many of these insects and flowers were mounted on coiled gold springs so that even the gentlest of movements resulted in a fluttering or scintillating effect. Known as *en tremblant*, the delicate trembling both allowed the gems to twinkle with little flashes of light and reinforced the realism of nature elegantly displayed in a man-made jewel.

Three late Victorian and turn of the century butterfly brooches. The example at the top is mounted with real butterfly wings under rock crystal, the centre is pavé diamond set and mounted en tremblant *to reinforce realism and the wings of the brooch at the bottom are set with panels of harlequin opal.*

(Below) Oval gold locket with pearl and diamond bunch of grapes surmount c.1880.

Diamond encrusted fly brooch, the 'abdomen' mounted with a fancy yellow diamond c.1885. Fancy diamonds were seen as interesting curiosities in the Victorian era; it is only in recent times that they have become so highly prized. Woolley & Wallis

Pavé-set pearl brooch modelled as a Faithful Hound. Mrs Vicky Waller

CHAPTER 11
JEWELS OF SENTIMENT AND LOVE

Jewellery, of all man-made objects, must surely represent the most tangible and enduring method of conveying long-term commitment and undying affection between friends and lovers. In its simplest form – a simple band of gold or metal – the tradition can be traced back to the Romans when a ring would be presented as a solemn pledge symbolising a formal contract or agreement between families. Hardly sentimental, but this practice ultimately led to the concept of giving an engagement ring representing a formal intention of betrothal before the wedding ceremony took place. The fashion for wearing wedding rings on the fourth finger of the left hand also has its origins in Roman times since it was believed that a nerve ran directly from there to the heart itself.

Throughout the Middle Ages and well into the 18th century, rings were made bearing a sentimental inscription or an affectionate message either within or engraved upon the surface of the hoop itself. These rings were collectively known as *posies* and appear on the market fairly regularly. Superficially, they look rather like plain gold wedding rings and thus can avoid detection unless examined carefully with a loupe. The inscriptions were usually in English, occasionally in French, and took the form of a simple verse such as 'God Above Increase Our Love' or 'In Thee A Flame – In Me The Same' or an intimate message on the lines of 'Joie Sans Fyn' (Joy Without End). The introduction of the Wedding Ring Act made hallmarks a compulsory feature in gold wedding bands and the fashion for posy rings quickly lapsed.

A form of betrothal ring popular in the 16th and 17th centuries was the *gimmel* named after Gemellus – a twin. Gimmel rings were composed of two identical hoops, usually enamelled and inscribed, which fitted together snugly but could be disconnected and worn separately by each partner. Two halves forming a whole was thus highly symbolic and it is perhaps surprising that the fashion for gimmels has been dormant for so long. Another romantic love token of the 18th and early 19th centuries was the *fede* or 'hand-in-hand' ring. Fede rings were generally made out of three separate hoops, either gold or silver, which were joined at the back by a tiny connecting rod which allowed the hoops to swivel. When fully closed, the top of a fedé ring shows two hands clasped together in friendship but when parted the hands reveal a miniature heart. This idea became particularly widespread in Ireland with the *claddagh* ring fashioned in the design of a heart flanked by two hands but in a single rigid construction.

An early 18th century gold posy ring. Delightfully intimate, these simple love tokens were engraved with a range of charming inscriptions.   S.J. Phillips

(Above) An early 19th century gold fede *or friendship ring in its closed position.*   S.J. Phillips

(Above right) The ring opened to reveal its construction of three flat gold bands pinned together at the back. The raised motif at the top of the centre hoop is a tiny gold heart.   S.J. Phillips

Heart-shaped diamond, ruby and enamel heart and coronet ring – an extremely desirable example of early 18th century sentimentality.
S.J. Phillips

Ruby, Oriental pearl and diamond twin heart and stylised bow ring c.1880. Care should be taken to ensure such rings are genuine and not modern reproductions.

Georgian ruby and diamond twin heart and coronet ring c.1800. Note the flat cutting of the gems, which would have been foiled to intensify their brilliance.

The combination of 'two hearts entwined' has been an enduringly popular design for rings and small brooches from the early 18th century to the present day. Superficially, their appearance has barely altered over the years; however, Georgian examples are decidedly prettier than their later counterparts, invariably set with cushion-shaped 'old-mine' diamonds and gems in fully enclosed backs which may exhibit engraved sunburst fluting. The shoulders of these earlier rings are often carved with rococo scrolls whilst the hearts themselves are further decorated with a bow or miniature coronet above. Victorian and later examples are altogether more flashy and 'harder' looking with tell-tale open backs, machined gold hoops and – needless to say – modern-cut gems.

The heart is unquestionably the most potent symbol of love used in all aspects of Victorian jewellery from brooches to lockets and bracelets to cufflinks.

Hearts were ideal for decorating in enamel – frequently sky-blue or navy – and later examples were

Gold bracelet mounted with a group of early 19th century gem-set gold lockets and locket back pendants. These pretty jewelled appendages were often decorated with three or four colour gold foliage.

(Above) Early 19th century gold friend-ship ring with a floral cluster of gems spelling 'REGARD'. Woolley & Wallis

(Top) Gold cannetille work dove brooch c.1825.

French early 19th century gold book vinaigrette locket c.1825.

(Above) Heart-shaped gold locket c.1825 with a cluster of gems, the first letter of each combining to spell the word REGARD. Popular designs included padlocks, hearts, keys and cupids. RBR Group at Grays

sometimes pavé-set with half pearls or rose diamonds. A most charming idea was particularly fashionable in the 1830s and 1840s where a heart-shaped locket was set with a line of coloured stones on a mount richly embellished with *trois couleur* or *quatre couleur* gold floral decoration. The initial letter of each stone spelled a message of intimacy such as REGARD (Ruby, Emerald, Garnet, Amethyst, Ruby, Diamond) or DEAREST. A miniature key attached to the suspension ring locked or unlocked the heart itself which might contain a woven plume of hair.

This idea of conveying intimacy was an important feature of early Victorian romantic jewellery with a wide range of sentimental subjects – cupids, arrows, keys, padlocks, anchors and bows – set with pretty gems (especially turquoise, pearl, ruby and diamond) in finely engraved gold settings decorated with twisted wire, beading and cannetille scrollwork.

Gold meshwork bracelet c.1830. This ravishing example is embellished with rubies and diamonds to the cuff, the hand and the hoop.

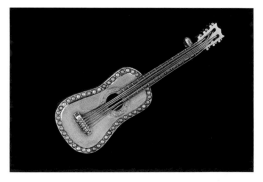

Early 19th century diamond-set novelty guitar brooch. These brooches usually contained a compartment for hair while vinaigrette lockets opened to reveal a pierced gold grille with a cavity underneath for a fragment of perfumed sponge.
Bentley & Skinner

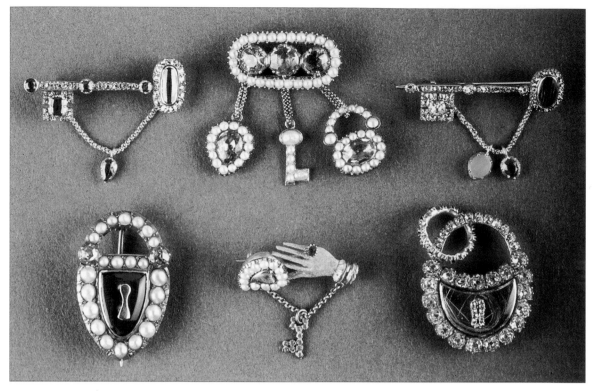

A group of highly sentimental Georgian diamond, enamel, half pearl and gem-set brooches exhibiting the range of designs popular at the time. The pink topaz and half pearl brooch at top centre is very typical.

Flowers suggested their own particular mood or sentiment; roses for happiness and love; ivy for friendship; broom for humility; turquoise for remembrance and pansy for dwelling in my thoughts. Late 18th and early 19th century French rings, brooches and seals were almost cloying with

(Left) Victorian gold and turquoise dove brooch carrying a spray of forget-me-nots in its beak, c.1845.

(Right) Pretty turquoise and gold locket ring containing a painted miniature, possibly Queen Victoria, c.1840.

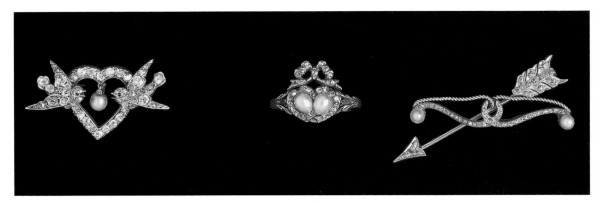

Three examples of late Victorian sentimental jewellery.

this sentimental ideal; cameos and intaglios depicted fat little putti, doves and lovebirds in tiny cages and lions harnessed to miniature chariots symbolising 'love tamed' or 'love trapped'.

Unswerving devotion was also the key feature of late 18th and early 19th century memorial jewellery in which classically-shaped brooches and rings contained under glass covers vignettes of ladies weeping tragically beside a plinth with urn surmount apparently containing the remains of the dear departed. Decorated with blue and white enamel, they were set with tiny rose diamonds or seed pearls symbolising tears and touchingly engraved with a suitable inscription on the back of the mounts.

Late Victorian Britain was deluged with a tidal wave of cheap and cheerful sentimental jewellery from silver 'name' brooches to little gold pins decorated with gem-set and half pearl flowers, horseshoes and birds – particularly swallows. Inexpensive engraved heart-shaped lockets fashioned in metal with gold 'fronts and backs' were made to contain a photograph or a lock of hair, while circular glass lockets in rims of gold or gilt might display the photograph of a brave young soldier off

to fight in the Boer Wars. Needless to say, the number of these evocative mementoes rose steeply during the early years of the First World War, as did Regimental bar brooches and patriotic 'emblem' pins such as bog-oak shamrock brooches and 'Good Luck' horseshoe pendants, stickpins and bangles.

Further reading

The Triumph of Love: Jewellery 1530-1950, Geoffrey C. Munn (Thames Hudson)

Victorian Jewellery, Margaret Flower (Cassell)

A History of Jewellery 1100-1870, Joan Evans (Faber & Faber)

Jewellery in Britain 1066-1837, Diana Scarisbrick (Michael Russell Publishing Ltd.)

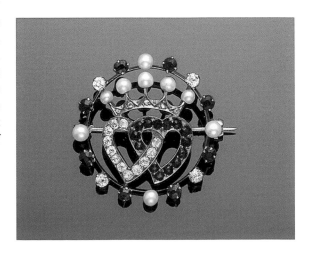

Late Victorian ruby, diamond and sapphire twin heart, coronet and hoop brooch in patriotic colours which coincided with the Diamond Jubilee of 1897.
Woolley & Wallis

105

CHAPTER 12
REVIVING HISTORY IN THE 19TH CENTURY

The Great Exhibition of 1851

For those successful, privileged and wealthy
Victorians living in Britain in the middle part of the
19th century, cultural life must surely have been a
grand and exciting experience. A burgeoning tourist
industry meant that people who had the means to do
so were travelling to European cities such as Paris,
Rome, Venice and Florence and further afield to
Athens and exotic Cairo to wonder at the astonishing

architecture and treasures of the Ancients. At the
same time intrepid explorers were bringing back
from their travels the art and merchandise of Africa,
Asia and the Orient. In 1851 a vast accumulation of
artefacts were assembled for 'The Great Exhibition
of the Industry of All Nations'. Here, in an area
covering nineteen acres in what was subsequently
known as the Crystal Palace, the wealth and cultural
diversity of the British Empire and beyond was put

The Poisoned Cup *by John Dawson Watson exhibiting a range of Gothic necklaces which would have been in fashion
in 1869, the year in which this watercolour was completed.* Private Collection/Bridgeman Art Library

on display for the benefit of well over six million visitors. Unsurprisingly, the Great Exhibition also gave scores of international jewellers a unique platform to show off their artistic creations inspired by themes as diverse as nature, archaeology, the Church, the Renaissance, the Middle Ages and Ancient Rome.

Classical Revivalism

Looking back 150 years, it is today a little difficult to comprehend the overwhelming fascination bordering on obsession felt by the Victorians for the rich treasures of the ancient world. Intrepid exploration had led to some amazing discoveries from the long forgotten civilisations of Assyria, Etruria, Mesopotamia and Greece, many of which were still in superb condition and extremely sophisticated in both design and execution. Soon the public were clamouring for jewellery which matched the breathtaking beauty of 2,000 year old Greek gold torcs, Roman collars and bracelets, Assyrian armlets and Etruscan earrings. The so-called *archaeological* jewellery of the 1860s and 1870s represented an extremely important development in the way gold was both fashioned and worn and also saw the success of a number of Italian, French and English goldsmiths who were key to the evolution of jewellery design in the 19th century.

Without doubt, the most celebrated of goldsmiths working in the archaeological style was Fortunato Pio Castellani (1793-1865). As early as the 1830s Castellani and his son Alessandro (1824-1883) had studied the lost art of the granulation mastered by the ancient Etruscan civilisation. This technique involved the application of thousands of tiny beads of gold on to a smooth surface which was further embellished with filigree wires soldered into coils and scrolls. Although Castellani never quite achieved the prowess of the ancient craftsmen, he certainly did manage to produce a superb range of bright yellow gold jewellery which, to reinforce the classical ideal, was often mounted with Roman or Greek coins, gem cameos or intaglios and Egyptian scarabs carved from hardstones such as cornelian and lapis lazuli. After F.P. Castellani died, the business was continued by Alessandro and his brother Augusto (1829-1914), selling an extensive output primarily from Naples as well as branches located in Paris and London. Considering the sheer quantity of pieces which were produced well into the 20th century, it is surprising that such a limited number appear on the market today; fine examples can easily fetch well into five figures although condition is an important consideration. The

(Left) Superior example of 19th century archaeological goldwork in a locket-back naturalistic pendant.

(Right) Castellani gold ram's head brooch with amphora drop c.1860.

(Far left) Archaeological gold earrings c.1860, their design faithful to the ancient ideal.
S.J. Phillips

(Left) Archaeological gold brooch by Castellani decorated with micromosaic tablet panels in three colours, c.1860.
S.J. Phillips

Castellani mark is a monogram of two entwined 'Cs' in back-to-back formation.

The classical ideal was embraced in motifs which brought to mind symbols easily associated with the ancients. Popular designs included the *amphora,* a vessel for holding wine which lent itself perfectly to drops on a necklace or pairs of earrings. The *bulla,* a type of round, hollow container, often depicted Latin words such as 'pax' or 'Roma', the *fibula* was a simple 'Roman' gold cloak fastener while Egyptian symbols such as lotus flowers, scarabs, pharoahs and the Sphinx were effortlessly adapted for use on

pendants and brooches by means of colourful and exotic micromosaic panels.

Leading contemporaries of Castellani are also celebrated for their accomplished gold work. Giacinto Melillo (1846-1915) initially studied as Castellani's pupil in the Naples workshop before setting up his own business specialising in intricate granulation on classical motifs such as the cornucopia and the putto. Ernesto Pierret (1824-1870) and Eugène Fontenay (1823-1887) both produced outstanding gold necklaces and pendants decorated with mosaic and enamel while John Brogden (active

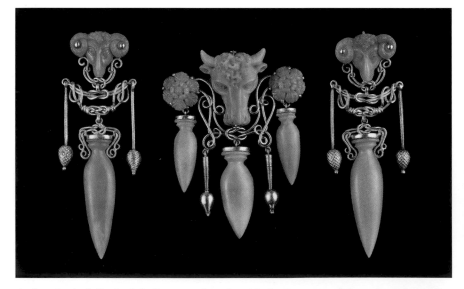

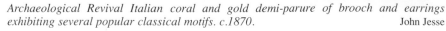

Archaeological Revival Italian coral and gold demi-parure of brooch and earrings exhibiting several popular classical motifs. c.1870.
John Jesse

Classical gold pendant, probably Italian c.1860.

(Far left) Pair of 19th century 'archaeological' micromosaic and gold earrings of Egyptian inspiration, Italian c.1865. Woolley & Wallis

(Left) John Brogden gold pendant in the Assyrian taste mounted with a fine hardstone cameo by Calabresi of Hercules wrestling the Nemean Lion. The cameo carved in around 1815 predates the frame by some sixty years. Note the tiny carved cameo heads where each of the 'bars' cross in the foreground.

1842-1855) was a London goldsmith who produced technically fine pieces, strongly Assyrian in influence, which incorporated fine cameos in gold frames decorated with colourful enamel or sturdy bangles and brooches mounted with eye-catching coral, turquoise and cabochons of almandine and pyrope garnet.

Gothic Revivalism

In exactly the same way as 19th century craftsmen revived the lost techniques and designs of ancient goldsmiths, so jewellers in England and France became fascinated with the art, culture and associated symbolism of the Middle Ages. Classical revivalist jewellery is nearly always set in bright yellow gold frames but, in keeping with the near-primitive output of the 13th and 14th century, many of the 19th century 'medieval' jewels are fashioned in silver set with extremely basic cabochon-cut gemstones or panels of coloured glass.

Gothic revivalism extended from the 1830s to the late 1890s. Much Berlin ironwork jewellery was strongly medieval in design and the black shiny metal lent itself admirably to themes which were

Bangle wrought to depict medieval rustics in bacchanalian revelry, a tour de force of French 19th century revivalist goldwork c.1870.

(Above) Gothic Revival necklace by Jules Wiese c.1860 exhibiting the firm's strong inclination towards using simple, almost primitive gems such as pale ruby and sapphire cabochons. The portraits are of medieval scholars.   S.J. Phillips

(Above left) A Gothic Revival quatrefoil-shaped brooch with strong ecclesiastical overtones c.1860.   S.J. Phillips

Eastern European enamel and silver George and Dragon pendant c.1895. Crudely finished, poorly enamelled and set with a pearl drop which is far too small for the size of the jewel, this is a prime example of sub-standard Gothic Revivalism.

clearly inspired by church architecture, angels and deities. François-Désiré Froment-Meurice (1802-1855) was a Parisian craftsman well known for ornate, three-dimensional bracelets and brooches fashioned in a combination of gold and oxidised silver which became known as the *style cathédrale*. Chivalry, the romance of the Arthurian legend, knights in shining armour and monstrous grotesques all strongly influenced craftsmen working in the Gothic taste; probably the two best known English designers were A.W.N. Pugin (1812-1852) and the architect William Burges (1827-1881) who both produced wonderfully evocative jewels in silver and gold which were plainly inspired by religious symbolism. Jules Wiese (1818-1890) and his son Louis (1852-1923) used simple gem cabochons such as ruby and sapphire in curiously distinctive hammered gold jewellery which was almost crude in its 'medieval' simplicity. This distinctive aspect of Wiese gold work is highly collectable today and correspondingly expensive. Towards the end of the century brightly coloured enamel, silver and gem-set pendants and necklaces became fashionable throughout Europe. So-called 'Austro-Hungarian' jewellery

(Above left) Wiese Gothic Revival silver panel bracelet. An extremely rare example since it is in its original cardboard box. S.J. Phillips

(Above right) Gold chimaera brooch grasping a diamond within its jaws. These 'broches-chimères' were popular in the 1870s and 1880s and were produced in both Germany and France. Woolley & Wallis

(Left) Gold ball and pedestal earrings in the classical taste c.1875. Victorian earrings are always desirable and the condition and elegant design of this pair would ensure a high price at auction. Woolley & Wallis

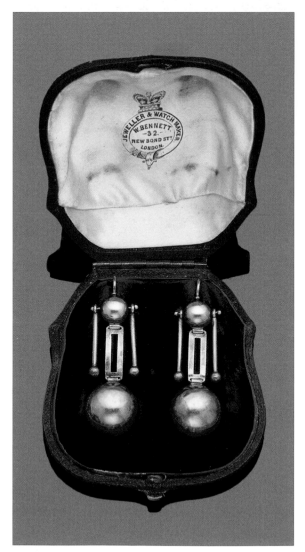

combines both Gothic and Renaissance themes using traditional and legendary subjects such as a 'Pelican in Piety' or 'St George slaying the Dragon'. Frequently crude, garish and extremely common, these Continental jewels can often be bought for less than £200.

Renaissance Revivalism

From around 1860 to 1880 several versatile jewellers began to work in a combination of two styles – neo-classical and neo-renaissance. The highly colourful and imaginative designs of the 16th and early 17th centuries inspired 19th century goldsmiths to create polychrome enamel and gold pendants, necklaces, brooches and earrings which were frequently set with hardstone cameos and a variety of semi-precious and precious gems in a range of styles which included galleons (called nefs), mythical beasts, classical deities, animals and birds.

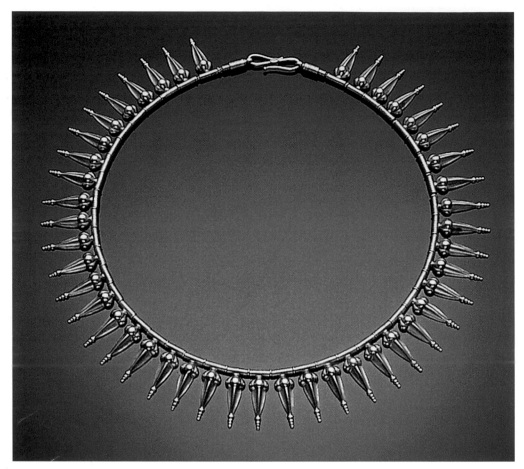

Carlo Giuliano gold archaeological fringe necklace c.1870. Giuliano was equally versatile in gold jewellery of classical inspiration or enamelled jewels in the Renaissance taste. Author's Collection

Pearls were particularly important in 19th century neo-renaissance jewellery. Just like their earlier counterparts, pendants were mounted with unusually shaped baroque pearls which could be cleverly set with little stones or embellished in gold to suggest, say, the body of an animal, a sea-serpent or a mermaid. These 19th century copies were sometimes so well crafted that they are extremely difficult to tell apart from earlier 'genuine' examples, a factor which has led to several well-documented – and quite acrimonious – disputes.

A popular variety of neo-renaissance gold work is the aptly named *Holbeinesque* jewel. Richly enamelled in several different colours and set with a com-bination of gems such as cabochon garnet and pale green chrysolite, these polychrome pendants and necklaces were made in the 1870s and are notable for their fine tracing of flowers and scrolls on the back of the frames. Neo-renaissance jewellery was largely inspired by the Romantic Movement which spread through Europe in the first half of the century. The goldsmith most closely associated with the fashion – and one of the most important figures in the world of antique jewellery – was Carlo Giuliano (1831-1895), a Neapolitan who trained under Castellani and subsequently settled in London where he opened a shop at 115 Piccadilly specialising in both classical and renaissance art jewels. Giuliano excelled in the

Colourful French Renaissance Revivalist necklace set with gems popular in this kind of inexpensive jewellery – garnets, citrines, turquoises, foiled crystal and amethyst.

(Left) 'Holbeinesque' neo-Renaissance emerald, diamond and enamel pendant c.1870.

(Right) Miniature of a lady in profile painted in around 1870. Note the Holbeinesque pendant of broadly similar design to the previous example.

Carlo Giuliano at his most accomplished. A set of gold necklace and earrings mounted with pyrope garnet and green enamel flowerheads with pearl and enamel fringe drops in between. Registered in November 1867.

(Opposite) C. & A. Giuliano opal and enamel pendant on a matching opal necklace in its original fitted case. c.1890.

application of enamel in beautifully wrought gold settings. The enamel itself was sometimes further decorated with little spots of a contrasting colour and the mounts were sympathetically matched with bouton pearls and gems notable for their reticence and character rather than their opulence and value. After Giuliano's death the aesthetic ideal was continued by his two sons, Carlo and Arthur, who produced wonderfully understated jewellery primarily enamelled in black and white. Carlo Giuliano's signature is the monogram 'CG' in an oval cartouche while later pieces are signed 'C & AG'. Care should

(Above) Robert Phillips gold and carbuncle garnet entwined brooch c.1870. 'Phillips of Cockspur Street' was celebrated for his use of coral and Italian shell cameos. He was also a champion of Carlo Giuliano whom he encouraged to open premises in London. S.J. Phillips

(Above right) The back of the garnet brooch showing the Phillips maker's mark.

be taken since signatures are easy to fake and are relatively common.

Robert Phillips (1810-1881) was another jeweller equally accomplished in neo-classical and neo-renaissance themes. 'Phillips of Cockspur Street', as he is generally known, produced fine archaeological gold work and is particularly associated with the use of coral which he adapted into fringe necklaces. He subsequently produced a series of 'Tudor' style gold cruciform pendants which, although similar to the work of Giuliano, are distinctive for their use of bold hardstones such as onyx. Robert Phillips signed his pieces with a stylised Prince of Wales feather motif in a shield or the monogram 'RP'. After his death in 1881 the business was taken over by his son, Alfred, who specialised in naturalistic gold scrolling pendants and brooches translucent enamelled in several vibrant colours and set with gems fashionable at the time such as opal, demantoid garnet and diamond.

Further reading

Castellani and Giuliano – Revivalist Jewellers of the 19th Century, Geoffrey C. Munn (Trefoil 1984)
Pre-Raphaelite to Arts and Crafts Jewellery, Charlotte Gere and Geoffrey C. Munn (Antique Collectors' Club)

Carlo Giuliano polychrome enamel, pearl and gold cruciform pendant of Renaissance inspiration. Giuliano's jewellery boxes are as beautifully constructed as their contents and will make a significant impact on value.
S.J. Phillips

CHAPTER 13
BASE METAL JEWELLERY AND MATERIALS

Cut Steel

Cut steel was an extremely effective variety of base metal jewellery, popular throughout the 18th and 19th centuries. Unlike paste, it was, on close inspection, difficult to confuse with diamonds. Nevertheless, it makes a significant impact when worn in artificial light and some of the superior examples of 18th century origin can be just as elegant and carefully constructed as expensive gem-set alternatives.

Cut steel can be traced as far back as the 16th century, although it was only in the mid-18th century that large quantities were produced commercially in England and France. The English cut steel industry was primarily located at Woodstock in Oxfordshire. Here many useful everyday accessories were made including chatelaines, buckles, buttons and watch chains with seals. Chatelaines were particularly compatible with steel: the shiny grey metal links looked business-like and they were strong and hard wearing, perfect for suspending below a variety of

(Above) French cut steel, blue glass and silver brooch c.1800. Note the number of facets on each individual stud, an indicator of early steel jewellery. Later steel may only exhibit five facets on each stud and is thus far cruder. Author's Collection

(Left) Two 18th century steel mesh bracelets with flower and quatrefoil-shape polished steel pailettes *together with a pair of earrings.* Linda Morgan

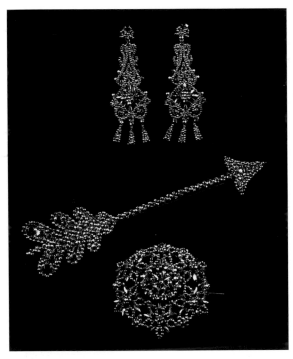

Typical 19th century cut steel.　　　　　Linda Morgan

(Below) Group of Victorian cut steel figurative brooches and buttons. Novelty designs such as the fish and the anchor will be more desirable than wreaths and clusters.
Mrs. Diana Foley

domestic appendages such as scissors, thimble, pencil and keys.

From the 1760s the vast majority of cut steel was manufactured at Soho near Birmingham. The leading producer was Matthew Boulton (1728-1809), an entrepreneurial industrialist better known for steam traction than dainty buttons and bows. Early cut steel was composed of clusters of small faceted and polished individual studs riveted on to a base plate. 18th century examples were sometimes composed of steel mesh with polished steel flowers and fancy quatrefoil-shaped plaques attached whilst, ever faithful to the neo-classical ideal, the studs were threaded in lines and mounted on broad clasps which were further enhanced by the addition of imitation pearls or jasperware plaques depicting mythological deities.

The tiny facets on each stud supplied the necessary glitter effect. 18th century steel exhibits up to fifteen facets on each stud whereas the mass-produced 19th century variety contains as few as five facets. Victorian cut steel is visibly coarser and cruder than its earlier counterpart and, needless to say, it is a lot less expensive. The two periods can be further differentiated by looking at the back of the object; whilst early steel exhibits individual hand-made rivets, the later machine-made variety does not.

Late 18th/early 19th century cut steel and mother-of-pearl necklace   Linda Morgan

Indeed, many later pieces are made from punched out metal strips betraying their 'factory' origin.

Necklaces and tiaras are particularly sought today. Necklaces often conformed to a popular design of star or flowerhead clusters (which sometimes revolved). Occasionally, long thin drops known as *pampilles* were suspended below. Bangles are quite common composed of four or five lines of studs in side-by-side formation. These were fastened by pressing a ball-shaped finial into a hole at the opposing end. Brooches were fashioned as circular clusters, stars or flowers. More interesting or novel designs such as butterflies, peacocks, fish, insects or Halley's comet will inevitably encourage higher prices. Earrings are rare and accordingly expensive.

The one great disadvantage of cut steel is its tendency towards rusting when left in a damp atmosphere. Rust is unsightly, invasive and difficult to remove without damaging the object itself.

Berlin Ironwork

The idea of a necklace composed of sections of black iron sounds, on the face of it, to be fairly uninspiring yet Berlin ironwork jewellery – particularly the elegant neo-classical pieces – offers the collector some of the prettiest and most intricate examples of the jeweller's art.

Precise origins of ironwork jewellery are unclear.

Two late 18th century/early 19th century ironwork neo-classical clasps, one in a cut steel frame.
RBR Group at Grays

Early 19th century Berlin iron mesh bracelet with clasp cast to depict Wellington and a delicate ironwork tracery brooch c.1815. Pat Novissimo

In the late 18th century a foundry at Gleiwitz in the Prussian province of Silesia specialised in the manufacture of a grey colour woven iron mesh of gossamer-like consistency. In 1804 a factory was established in Berlin for the production of iron objects, both functional and decorative, known as the Royal Berlin Factory. Jewellery represented only a fraction of total production which included small-scale practical objects such as buckles, keys, tinder boxes and purses to massive-scale industrial output encompassing gates, grilles, balustrades and bridges.

The development of ironwork jewellery as a distinct commodity really began to take off between the years 1813 to 1815 as a response to a general plea by the Prussian authorities for members of the aristocracy to 'donate' their gold and jewels for the war effort against Napoleon. Appealing to patriotism tapped perfectly into the psychology of the people, since in exchange for gold jewellery they were given ironwork necklaces, crosses, brooches and bracelets, sometimes bearing the emotive inscription 'Gold gab ich für Eisen' (I gave gold for iron) or 'eingetauscht

Two early 19th century ironwork bracelets combining neo-classical and Gothic themes.
Madeleine C. Popper

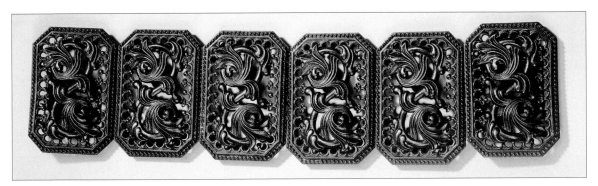

A fine Berlin ironwork panel bracelet by Geiss of ornate Gothic design together.

RBR Group at Grays

zum Wohle des Vaterlandes' (exchanged for the welfare of the Fatherland). To get some idea of the scale of production, over 41,000 items of jewellery were made in 1814 alone.

Berlin iron jewellery was produced by shaping wax moulds into the desired design and enclosing them in iron boxes packed with with sand. Once the mould had been removed, molten iron was poured into the remaining cavity. After it had cooled down, the object was removed from its sand impression for cleaning and hand finishing. The application of a varnish made of linseed oil and white pitch protected against rusting; a coat of black lacquer gave further protection and provided an attractive patina.

Jewellery passed through several strongly contrasting and recognisable styles. From about 1800 to 1820 neo-classicism predominated; thus a typical necklace would be composed of a series of oval plaques delicately wrought to depict mythological deities, nymphs, putti and songbirds connected together by several tiers of fine link chains or gauze-like mesh. Occasionally the plaques were set in thin rims of gold or the mesh was embellished with steel stars or sequins known as *paillettes*.

From about 1815 to 1830 neo-classicism gave way to naturalism in which flowers, leaves and butterflies were the guiding theme. A popular design for bracelets and necklaces was a scallop or ivy-shaped leaf delicately pierced to suggest the leaf's veins and stem. From the 1830s onwards a heavier Gothic style entered general use characterised by sections of ornate tracery and complicated cartouche or quatre-foil patterns more associated with church architecture than dainty jewels. Gothic ironwork might be designed as elaborate pillars with ornate scrolls and figures of saints.

After around 1850 the popularity of Berlin ironwork rapidly receded although it was also sold as mourning jewellery in France from the 1820s. There are several prominent manufacturers whose work is particularly sought; probably the best known are Johann Conrad Geiss, who was active in the 1830s, and Devaranne, who showed iron jewellery at the 1851 Great Exhibition.

A superb ironwork necklace of scallop-shaped sections by Geiss, c.1820-30.

Madeleine C. Popper

Marcasite

Although marcasite is well known today for its abundant use in affordable and decorative 20th century jewellery, its origins can actually be traced back as far as the 18th century when it was set in inexpensive accessories such as buttons and buckles as well as cheap but pretty items of silver jewellery.

Marcasite is iron pyrites – sometimes called 'fool's gold' – which has been faceted to give it its characteristic yellowish-grey glitter. This means that it is routinely confused with cut steel, a problem compounded by the fact that it was frequently used in late 18th or early 19th century neo-classical jewellery as a border to jasperware plaques, 'Coq de Perle' necklaces or cobalt blue glass copying much more expensive blue enamel.

Aluminium

Summed up by the expression 'light and white', aluminium was a rare and expensive commodity during the 19th century and much of the jewellery was heavily influenced by Gothic revivalism. The surface of the metal was invariably chased with elaborate scrolls and the hard white colour of the material was also always offset by yellow gilt metal

Art Nouveau gunmetal cigarette case with silver high-lights.   RBR Group at Grays

backing plates and mounts. Modern aluminium jewellery is sometimes given a delicate tinted surface by a procedure known as anodising.

Gunmetal

Gunmetal was extensively used in late 19th century accessories such as mesh purses, chatelaines, cigarette cases and vesta boxes as well as assorted jewellery, chains and the cases of fob watches. The material exhibits a characteristic blue-black colour and satin-like sheen which could be an ideal contrast to gemstones or even small diamonds. It was popular in Russia, Germany and Austria, but its tendency towards rusting and general deterioration considerably affects its value.

Pinchbeck

An alloy of zinc and copper invented by Christopher Pinchbeck (1672-1732), a clock- and watchmaker of Fleet Street, it appeared to all intents and purposes exactly like gold and was used in its own right in the manufacture of robust belcher link muff chains, pairs of mesh bracelets and long decorative earrings, as well

Japanese shakudo work brooch c.1870. Originally used in sword mounts, shakudo was a cast alloy of gold and copper which was then decorated with gold and silver Oriental motifs such as birds and flowers.   RBR Group at Grays

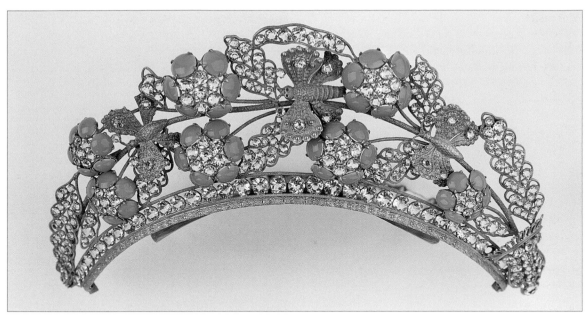

Early Victorian pinchbeck and turquoise-blue glass tiara c.1830. This elegant floriate spray is further set with colourless paste and three butterflies in flight.
Sandra Cronan

Pinchbeck muff chain, c.1825, with a typical Georgian clasp.
Mrs. Diana Foley

123

as an accompaniment to bold coloured agates and hardstones in brooches and necklaces.

In the 19th century it was fashionable to remove the pinchbeck 'watchcocks' from the movements of pocket watches and mount them together into rather effective necklaces in which no two watchcocks are identical.

Pinchbeck should not be confused with later, inferior gilt metal which usually discolours after prolonged use.

Further reading

Cut-Steel and Berlin Iron Jewellery, Anne Clifford (Adams & Dart)

Victorian Jewelry: Unexplored Treasures, Ginny Redington Dawes and Corinne Davidov (Abbeville Press Publishers)

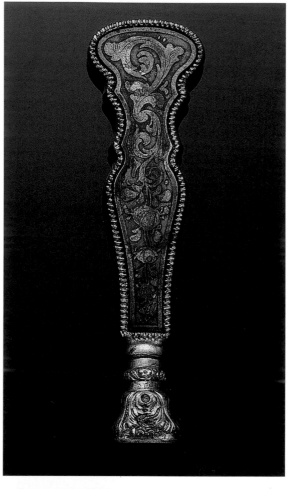

(Right) Pinchbeck desk seal encasing an ironwork pedestal decorated with scrolls c.1800. Woolley & Wallis

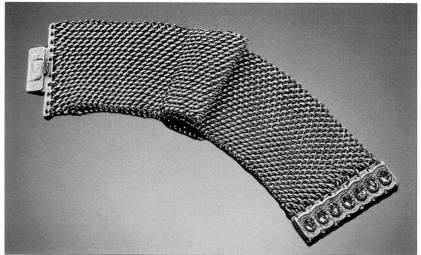

(Left) Pinchbeck mesh bracelet c.1825. Such bracelets are often fashioned in pairs with clasps set with coloured pastes or banded agate.
Brian and Lynn Holmes

(Opposite) A colourful collection of inexpensive English butterfly brooches enamelled on silver and metal, first half of the 20th century.
John Jesse

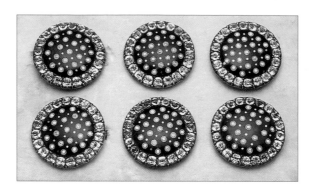

CHAPTER 14
PERIOD ACCESSORIES AND FUNCTIONAL JEWELLERY

Shoe Buckles

If you are thinking of starting a collection of antique jewellery, you could do far worse than begin with a few Georgian buckles. Reasonably common and surprisingly cheap, buckles were an obligatory accessory for both men's and women's footwear throughout the 18th century.

The frames of Georgian buckles were usually oval or rectangular in shape and were curved to fit over the instep. The central section, known as the chape and composed of the pin and tongue, was invariably made of steel. Matthew Boulton, famous for his

pioneering work in cut steel, was also a prominent buckle-maker.

Buckles made during the 1720s-1750s were often composed of engraved silver frames while examples made between 1750 and 1800 were generally set with paste. Colourless paste buckles are extremely common and coloured paste is considerably rarer, while unusual materials, such as earthenware, tin and French jet (black glass), can still be found in 'box lots' at auction.

The major problem with buckles is that they are impractical for wearing nowadays. Some have been converted into brooches but this reduces the value. Another problem is the difficulty in finding matched pairs, as you might expect with an accessory subjected to robust everyday use 250 years ago. Identical pairs are, therefore, very collectable especially if lodged in their original fitted boxes.

Buttons

Buttons are keenly sought today and fine quality 18th century sets of six or twelve can fetch several hundreds or even thousands of pounds. Buttons were

Set of six Georgian colourless paste and royal blue enamel buttons with gold spot and white enamel polka dot decoration. English c.1825. Private Collection

Three pairs of buckles. The two upper pairs are late 18th century, the bottom pair 19th century. Robust for everyday use, they were invariably lost or divided, thus pairs in good condition are far more commercial than odd singletons. Sandra Cronan

manufactured from a large and varied number of materials, usually of a fairly modest value, while gold and gem-set buttons can be traced from the 17th century through to the 1920s and 1930s when firms such as Cartier produced elegant platinum, gold, diamond and jewelled buttons to match pairs of cufflinks and dress studs.

A complete set is absolutely vital since the loss of a solitary component will reduce the value quite significantly – a fitted box containing eleven buttons and one gap is extremely vexing and near-impossible to remedy.

Among the many designs used for antique buttons, some of the more common examples include early 18th century dome-backed silver 'ball' designs set with colourless paste imitating diamond; clusters of cut steel (produced in very large numbers during the 18th and 19th centuries); gilt metal rococo plaques decorated with colourful enamel 'romantic' landscapes and novelty subjects which were mass-produced from the 1890s onwards.

Perhaps the prettiest and most desirable period for collectors today is Art Nouveau in which the individual buttons were decorated with flowers or perhaps embossed with a female head which was further embellished in green and blue enamel. Signed sets by Liberty, Charles Horner or Murrle Bennett are especially prized. Condition, as always, is crucial.

Lorgnettes

The French word *lorgnette* broadly embraces a group of functional accessories including miniature spy glasses fashionable at the opera and the theatre in the 18th century and lorgnettes used for reading. Quizzing glasses were composed of a single lens and were worn at the end of a long chain or ribbon. Lorgnettes enjoyed widespread use in the 19th century; inexpensive examples were made of silver, gilt metal, gunmetal and tortoiseshell, while superior

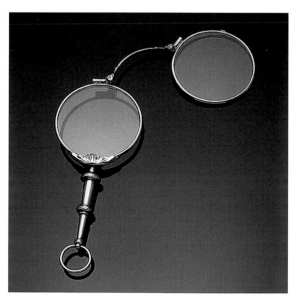

Pair of early Victorian gold sprung lorgnettes c.1845 with coloured gold decoration. S.J. Phillips

Pair of silver lorgnettes c.1910 decorated with green and violet four leaf clovers. The colours suggest this may possibly have been made for a follower of the Suffragette movement. Sylvie Spectrum

Fine neo-classical gold chatelaine c.1800 set with blue glass plaques and suspending a watch with accompanying key and seal. Bentley & Skinner

vast majority of lorgnettes were opened by retraction of a small cylinder or compression of a lever causing the lens to spring open. Progressive use weakens the mechanism and can affect value.

Chatelaines

The most practical of all 'everyday' accessories, chatelaines were popular from the early 18th century through to the end of the 19th century when their use became purely functional rather than decorative.

Chatelaines were composed of a gold, silver, steel or gilt metal shield-shaped hook inserted into the belt from which was suspended a series of matching chains, each with a useful appendage such as étui, scissors, fob watch, pomander or miniature purse. Fine examples made in the 18th century were mounted in three- or four-colour gold chased with repoussé decoration and studded with gems. Fine French chatelaines were enamelled with pretty scenes and landscapes while the fob watch was accompanied by a matching watch key and seal. 18th century pinchbeck chatelaines often suspended several needlework appendages, but finding complete sets with the contents fully intact is extremely unusual.

Seals

Seals can be divided into two principal categories: fob seals – small and practical accessories worn on a watch chain or as an appendage to a chatelaine – and desk seals which were, as you might expect, larger, more imposing and kept for sealing documents, usually of a legal or formal nature.

Seals are among the earliest artefacts which can be traced back in civilised history composed of materials such as faience and basalt and fashioned into cylindrical shapes suitable for rolling on wax. Simple and fairly crude medieval seals, often mistaken for later examples, were made from silver or metal while mid-18th century 'Jacobite' fob seals in steel, the base engraved with a head or coat of arms, are fairly common. Occasionally the 'business-end' of the seal could be made to swivel – a feature of some Victorian seals where a semi-precious stone, usually citrine, was engraved on three faces with a coat of arms, a family crest and the owner's monogram.

models were fashioned in three or four colour gold embellished with gems such as ruby, turquoise and pearl. Fabergé produced a range of lorgnettes with enamelled stems, while Cartier and French jewellers before the First World War made elegant lorgnettes in platinum set with clusters of small diamonds. The

Mid- to late 18th century seals are characteristic for their classical austerity. The pedestal, or handle, was usually of a stylised bell-shape and typical of the prevailing taste; the base took the form of a foil-backed amethyst, citrine or rock crystal or a hard-stone such as cornelian, onyx or chalcedony, carved with a head in profile. In keeping with the fashion for sentiment at the start of the 19th century, seals were smaller, prettier and elaborately embossed in several different colours of gold. The hardstone stamp was engraved with a suitably feminine device such as doves in flight and a simple expression of affection such as 'amitie' or 'pour vous.' These seals were often further embellished with little gems, particularly rubies, turquoises and half pearls, and it was not unknown to place a locket compartment in the base for containing hair.

Victorian seals are extremely common and variable in quality. Many were strengthened for everyday use by adding a core of metal and care should be taken to ensure that a seal called 'gold' is indeed as described. Many seals made from the 1840s to 1860s were simply gilt metal with glass bases and are, quite frankly, extremely crude, whilst late 19th century seals were invariably nine carat gold mounted with two predictable hardstones – cornelian and bloodstone. Seals such as these were worn on the end of a gold watch chain and are realistically priced today.

As pocket watches gave way to wristwatches, the fashion for wearing fob seals on the end of alberts also faded so that by around 1910 production more or less evaporated. Today, nine carat gold 'Victorian style' seals are produced to be worn on charm bracelets or as decorative pendants. Modern seals usually exhibit identifying hallmarks.

Blackamoor Seals and Musical Seals

Two interesting varieties in use in the 18th and 19th centuries were seals in which the pedestal was carved to represent the head and body of a blackamoor or Nubian princess and gold seals which contained a miniature mechanism which, when fully wound, played a pretty tune. Blackamoor seals were often studded with little gems such as diamonds in

(Above) Gold seal with coiled serpent pedestal and revolving wheel set with a series of foiled semi-precious gems. These pretty jewelled seals anticipated more robust, workmanlike desk seals used in business and legal transactions from the 1840s onwards.   S.J. Phillips

(Above right) Rare gold seal modelled as a native beehive. Contained within is a lock of hair and an inscription stating that it was removed from Napoleon at St. Helena on 22 July 1819. This is particularly poignant since bees were Napoleon's personal symbol.

Series of miniature gold seals and a matching watch key suspended from a Georgian embossed gold split ring c.1825-1830.   Woolley & Wallis

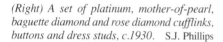

(Above) Early 19th century gold musical seal with enamelled erotic study concealed within the base. Clearly an amusing conversation piece for a dilettante gentleman. French c.1800. S.J. Phillips

(Right) A set of platinum, mother-of-pearl, baguette diamond and rose diamond cufflinks, buttons and dress studs, c.1930. S.J. Phillips

the eyes or rubies in the hair while musical seals might contain a hidden compartment with an erotic scene within which, to put it delicately, the figures performed in time to the music.

Cufflinks

Demand for elegant and colourful Victorian and later cufflinks has shot up in recent years and gone are the days when a pair of 'turn of the century' diamond-set enamelled cufflinks could be bought at auction for less than £250. A primary factor is that cufflinks offer collectors one of the few areas of jewellery readily available (and socially acceptable) to men. Today most high street menswear shops sell a wide range of silver, gilt and enamel cufflinks contributing to a greater awareness and appreciation of the discipline and intensifying demand for good quality pairs which appear in the salerooms or which are sold in specialist shops.

The two important aspects which must be borne in mind when buying period cufflinks are *design* and *condition*. A pair of Edwardian nine carat gold oval plaque cufflinks will certainly do the job for which they were intended but are stylistically repetitive, while a pair with, say, chipped enamel, worn settings

and connections falling apart are frankly more of a liability than an asset.

The fashion for wearing cufflinks can be traced back to the early 18th century when pairs of rock crystal mounted 'Memento Mori' buttons were joined together in silver; in Scotland polished agate or hardstone plaques were similarly constructed in extremely simple settings. Victorian and Edwardian gold cufflinks, usually fifteen or eighteen carat, were made in a wide range of designs. It is, however, those subjects which are described as 'novelty' or inspired by a specific theme such as sport, hunting or nature which are most desirable today. Thus, diamond studded foxheads, enamelled gamebirds or freshwater fish will predictably appeal to sporting enthusiasts while amusing designs such as enamelled skulls and crossbones or 'ruination' cufflinks, enamelled to depict the four gentlemen's vices of drink, cards, racehorses and easy women, are enduringly popular.

The vintage era for cufflink production was the first thirty years of the 20th century when jewellers such as Cartier and Tiffany produced elegant and highly original examples in a range of materials set in gold and the versatile new metal which was

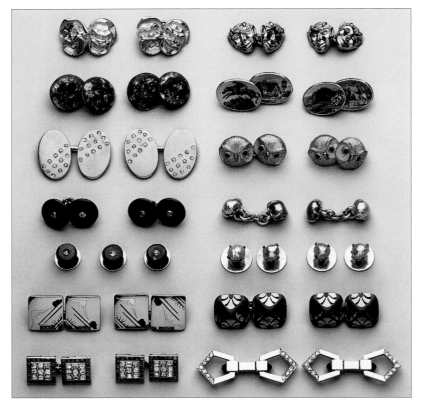

Pair of Fabergé blue chalcedony and enamel cufflinks c.1900. Bentley & Skinner

A group of gold, platinum and gem set cufflinks, dates ranging from c.1880-1925. A good example of the sheer diversity of designs. The general guideline with cufflinks is the more unusual or novel the subject, the greater the value. Thus, the 'grotesque' cufflinks at top left are exceedingly commercial while a standard pair of late Victorian 9 carat gold oval plaques are broadly worth the value of the gold. Sandra Cronan

revolutionising jewellery construction – platinum. Using platinum as well as gold could provide craftsmen with limitless opportunities of creating intricate and innovative designs in all sorts of fancy patterns set with gemstones and hardstones cut into suitably compatible shapes. Van Cleef & Arpels and Cartier, for example, produced distinctive square 'chequerboard' cufflinks with matching dress studs invisibly set with diamonds, rubies and sapphires, while Fabergé sold diamond, gem-set and enamel cufflinks in tasteful neo-classical shapes from his shops in St Petersburg, Moscow and London.

It was a natural progression for complete sets of accessories comprising cufflinks, buttons and dress studs to be made for gentlemen wearing formal attire; less expensive examples common from the 1920s to the war years were composed of mother-of-pearl discs or plaques bordered by onyx or enamel and set in nine carat white and yellow gold or silver. These sets were nearly always sold in neat fitted boxes, an aspect

which certainly increases value, although the loss of a single component reduces appeal.

Cufflinks have always been both functional and, at the lower end of the market, cheap; mass-produced examples in nine carat gold, silver or gilt metal are extremely common. The majority of gold cufflinks made from the 1890s to the 1920s were usually fashioned in oval, circular or torpedo shapes, were elaborately engraved and bear a full set of hallmarks.

Do inspect cheaper cufflinks with great care for indications of later repair and dents. Damage to enamel is often concealed by 'cold painting' but it is near impossible to match the original patina. Some cufflinks are quite simply four buttons which have been recently 'joined up', so check that the connecting chains are original. Finally, examine any makers' marks extremely carefully. A Russian '56' stamp, a French gold 'eagle head' control mark or an individual series of numbers on the edge of the setting can increase value substantially.

Tiepins

Unlike cufflinks, tiepins (also known as scarf pins or stickpins) are seldom worn today and tend to be bought by collectors for their novelty or rarity value. Tiepins were very much a 19th and early 20th century feature. Indeed, during the last quarter of the 19th century, an enormous number were produced to be worn on ties or cravats of which the vast majority are, to put it bluntly, extremely dull with uninspiring designs ranging from simple crescents, horseshoes and flowerheads set with little pearls or cheap gems to embellished gold plaques sometimes set with a small diamond. It is only when the subject matter or the gemstones featured start to be interesting that prices for tiepins rise sharply. The evidence of a signature – particularly Fabergé or Cartier – will certainly heighten demand.

18th century tiepins were altogether smaller and daintier than later examples. The pin itself was generally twisted in the centre to form one of several interesting shapes such as a zig-zag or a coil. The head of these Georgian pins was usually pretty basic, nothing more than a cushion-shaped paste, a coloured gem such as a ruby or garnet or a rose diamond in a gold collet setting. Late 18th century tiepins were rather similar to the rings fashionable at that time – a floral cluster of gems, a hardstone in a border of garnets or a sentimental 'In Memoriam' subject such as a sepia painted weeping lady in a border of seed pearls or enamel.

19th century tiepins were extraordinarily diverse utilising a wide and varied range of materials. The themes largely paralleled whatever was fashionable at the time – thus when neo-classicism was the dominant style tiepins faithfully conformed with hardstone, shell and coral cameos carved with the heads of deities in profile. Nature and naturalism, always key to Victorian jewellery, was observed in coiled snakes enamelled in blue surrounding a diamond or a pearl, while birds of prey such as eagles or falcons were carved from gold or set with turquoises. A recurring theme from the 1860s to the 1880s was the reverse crystal intaglio in which a

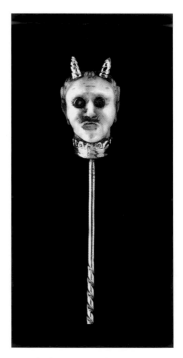

Jewelled 'Devil' stick pin. Novelties and 'theme' subjects such as sport and politics will always attract keen interest. Bentley & Skinner

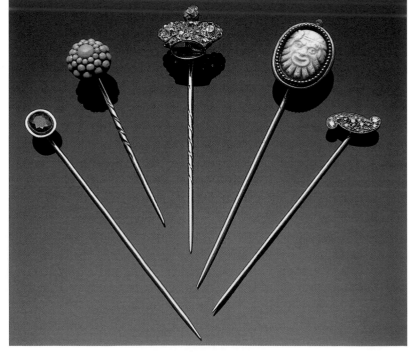

Group of tiepins, dates ranging from c.1860 to 1920. Note the fancy blue diamond example, extreme right. Tiepins offer an excellent way to start collecting rare and unusual gemmological specimens. S.J. Phillips

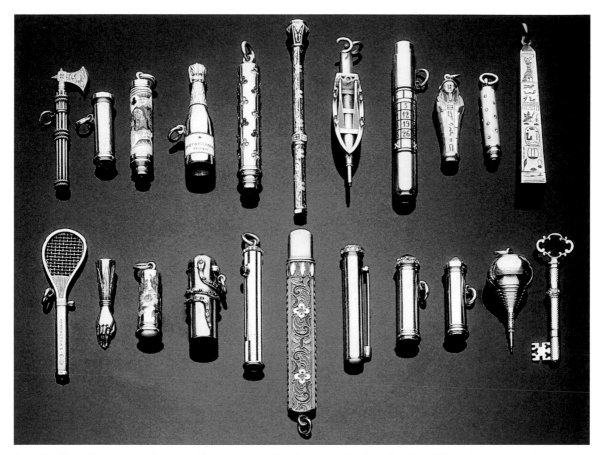

Pencils offer collectors an almost limitless resource of designs, ranging from functional Victorian combinations of pens with pencils to novelty subjects such as the champagne bottle and spinning top illustrated above. The best known maker was Sampson Mordan & Co. and most examples were constructed with a 'telescopic' mechanism, extending their length to twice or three times their normal size.

domed plaque of rock crystal was engraved at the back and painted with the design of an animal or a bird – domestic pets such as tabby cats and pug dogs particularly appealed to Victorian sentiment. Insects, especially jewelled house flies, beetles and spiders, were keenly collected along with all manner of sporting and recreational subjects which, by the 1890s, played such an important role in people's everyday lives.

Just like cufflinks, the prime factor affecting the value of tiepins is novelty and originality so, whereas a diamond foxhead, diamond pheasant or enamel flag will certainly be collectable, a rare or amusing subject such as a diamond bicycle, a fully articulated enamel clown or a pin with a political message will achieve a far higher price.

By the early 20th century, tiepins were fashioned in platinum as well as gold and motifs were usually gem set, from the single drop-shaped Oriental pearl to interesting fancy-cut diamond and gem-set novelties by Cartier and Boucheron, such as a miniature yacht set with triangular diamond 'sails'. These tiepins are highly sought and can easily fetch well into the thousands, especially if the diamonds are in a combination of fancy colours underlining the 'novelty' factor so important to tiepin buyers.

A further group of 'turn of the century' tiepins are illustrated on page 60.

Pocket Watches and Fob Watches

Pocket watches with their accompanying chains, commonly known as Alberts, turn up at auction with relentless frequency. The vast majority of gold and silver pocket watches fetch prices commensurate with their smelt value so when we consider the price of many modern sport or fashion wristwatches on the market today, a fine old Victorian timepiece really can represent a solid and reassuring investment at a reasonably modest outlay. Gentlemen's pocket watches were invariably worn in the waistcoat pocket at the end of a chunky gold or silver chain while smaller, daintier ladies' fob watches were clipped to the end of a long guard chain or were suspended from a matching brooch, usually of tied bow design and worn on the blouse or jacket.

The majority of pocket watches at the end of the 19th century contained keyless lever movements in hunter or half hunter cases. These outer covers were often engraved with a monogram or flowers; better quality gold examples repeated the quarters or the minutes. The dials were invariably enamelled white with black Roman or arabic numerals. Many old dials betray fine hairline cracks so close inspection is recommended since damage reduces value considerably. American manufacturers such as Waltham and Elgin produced large numbers of gold plated pocket watches which are often mistaken for gold. A signature will make a significant difference to the potential value of any timepiece. Prominent makers' names include Patek Philippe, Cartier, Rolex and Vacheron Constantin.

Generally speaking, fob watches from the early part of the 20th century are more interesting and valuable

Late Victorian long gold guard chain c.1895. These were sometimes strengthened by adding inner 'secret' rings within the gold links. Note the '9 c' plaque above the fitting.
Sylvie Spectrum

Group of 9 carat gold, silver and gilt metal gentlemen's and ladies' pocket watches c.1900 together with a bar link and a curb link 9 carat gold watch chain. Sylvie Spectrum; Don Wood

Regency gold vinaigrette c.1825 mounted above and below with covers of golden citrine. Vinaigrettes played an important role in Georgian towns and cities. Containing perfumed sponges, they were held to the nose and kept the vile odours of the street at bay.

Woolley & Wallis

(Above) Lady's gold, enamel and half pearl fob watch suspended from a matching bow brooch c.1880. Inexpensive and plentiful, the mechanisms of these fobs were pretty basic while constant use often resulted in visible damage.　　　　Woolley & Wallis

(Above right) Fine quality Cartier platinum, enamel, diamond and pearl fob watch with 'Indo-Persian' enamel cover c.1912.　　　　Sandra Cronan

than the standard gold models in production during the Victorian era. Edwardian and Belle Époque fob watches are frequently enamelled in pretty translucent colours and are sometimes decorated with a geometric cluster of small diamonds or a line of half pearls to the bezels. These small but extremely elegant timepieces were occasionally accompanied by matching chains interspaced with 'batons' – or a series of cylinders enamelled in compatible colours to the watch itself. Probably the best known manufacturer of fob watches was the French firm Le Roy et Fils who invariably signed their products upon the inner gold cover.

Further reading

Chatelaines – Utility to Glorious Extravagance by Genevieve E. Cumming and Nerylla D. Taunton (Antique Collectors' Club, 1994)

Understanding Jewellery by David Bennett and Daniela Mascetti (Antique Collectors' Club, 2003)

Amusing asymmetric silver and enamel minaudière featuring a caricature of Enrico Caruso c.1925. Minaudières were multi-purpose vanity cases popular from the 1930s to the 1950s. Containing compartments for mirror, lipstick, comb, cigarettes, money and even a watch, they quickly became an indispensable accessory for women in society.

John Jesse

CHAPTER 15
SILVER JEWELLERY

Whilst *Starting to Collect Antique Jewellery* is most definitely not a study of antique silver and plate – for that please refer to Ian Pickford's companion title in this series – it is still important to recognise the critical role which silver has played in the history of jewellery design.

Silver Settings

During the 16th century nearly all 'high' jewellery – jewels for the rich and powerful – was constructed entirely from gold, and high carat gold at that. With the gradual development of diamond cutting and gem polishing in the 17th century, expensive gold gave way to cheaper and infinitely more practical silver.

By far the most common method of retaining a gem in its mount was the *collet,* a technique which remained fashionable right up to the end of the 19th century when platinum radically changed the way in which stones were set in jewellery. A collet is a box-shaped surround which tightly grips the stone in place. Collets are often referred to as 'cut down setting' since the box is quite literally cut down to expose the stone to the light.

17th and 18th century jewels set in silver were invariably fully enclosed at the back of the mount so that no light could penetrate through the gemstone itself. This meant that poorly cut diamonds and simple coloured gems could often appear extremely dull and lifeless and led to the development of *foiling* in which metal tinfoil of compatible colour was placed behind the stone to enhance sparkle and reflect back light through the top. Many 18th century rings are composed of a single gem or series of gems which are set in silver, fully enclosed at the back in gold or silver gilt and foiled to appear like, for instance, ruby or sapphire – although the true identity of the gem may be nothing more valuable than rock crystal or paste. It was not until the 19th century that jewellery was mounted in gold and set in silver but left fully open at the back so that all the available light could pass through the stones.

Silver Jewellery

The explosion in the manufacture of decorative silver jewellery was very much a 19th century phenomenon, generated in no small part by the discovery of the Comstock Lode in Nevada, USA, in around 1860. By the 1870s European markets were flooded with cheap and wearable silver necklaces, bracelets and brooches which could be produced inexpensively and purchased for a matter of shillings, so making silver available to a universal

---

(Above) Emerald and diamond flower spray brooch c.1750. During the 18th century the majority of gems were set in cut-down silver collets and were fully enclosed at the back of the mount. S.J. Phillips

Banded agate and silver cylindrical cross on an onyx ball chain c.1880.
Ginny Redington Dawes

Group of silver lockets and collars c.1885.
Brian and Lynn Holmes

public which simply could not afford expensive gold and gem-set alternatives. Another added bonus of silver was that it could be gilded to look like gold. Silver gilt jewellery – chains, lockets and necklaces – are actually quite difficult to tell from old gold examples and even today cause endless confusion for dealers, shops and auction houses.

In Scotland production of silver jewellery had become firmly established by the 18th century. Frequently functional rather than purely decorative, silver plaid brooches mounted with large foiled crystals or coloured quartz pinned coarse fabric while ring brooches – flat hoops with open centres – were given as betrothal gifts. In the late 18th and 19th centuries pretty brooches fashioned as two entwined hearts were sold as Good Luck tokens. Called luckenbooths, they were so described because they

were sold in locked booths around St Giles' Kirk, Edinburgh.

English mid-19th century jewellery manufacturers such as Ellis & Sons of Exeter and George Unite of Birmingham produced easy to wear silver brooches of a strongly figurative design such as the 'safety' brooch fashioned as a broad knot or scroll with floral chasing and a spherical drop below. Brooches were indeed extremely popular throughout the 19th century. Another fashionable style was the outstretched hand or a woodland image of acorns and leaves. The most recognisable design for silver jewellery in the 1870s and 1880s was the collar with matching locket suspended below. These highly versatile combinations looked particularly striking when worn on black and a testament to their popularity is the number which are readily available

Silver brooch mounted with a Webb's cameo glass plaque, English c.1870.   John Jesse

Group of four broad Victorian silver cuff bangles c.1880, two with gold overlay decoration. Buckles and straps were ideal designs for this type of bracelet which remained popular well into the 20th century.
Brian and Lynn Holmes

today. Composed of broad, articulated mesh or a series of uniform panels, the lockets of matching design were suspended from enlarged integral bolt rings and fittings.

In 1854 a treaty was signed between America and Japan which triggered a craze for all things Oriental. Greater co-operation between East and West resulted in a deluge of art, textiles, lacquerwork and metalwork flooding into Europe. In terms of silver jewellery, this obsession with Japanese culture stimulated the development of the *Japonaiserie* style in which the overwhelming influence was Nature presented with understated Oriental simplicity. The polished surface of silver bangles, for instance, would be engraved with a landscape containing swallows in flight, delicate flowers, waterlilies and clumps of bamboo. Brooches were similarly engraved and overlaid with pink or yellow gold floral 'highlights', a technique visually effective and in fashion right up to the end of the century.

The trend towards minimalism and underplayed decoration was not only confined to jewellery but embraced most aspects of the decorative arts – and not just in Britain but throughout Europe and America. This appreciation and application of all things elegant and beautiful was termed *Aestheticism* and was a crucial factor in the development of the Art Nouveau movement.

By the 1880s remorseless mass-production of cheap and modest silver jewellery resulted in a near total collapse of the market. In 1887 the Birmingham Jewellers' and Silversmiths' Association was established to promote the cause of the industry which slowly began to prosper once more with the manufacture of inexpensive 'sweetheart' brooches and associated trinkets. Machine-made and cut from sheet silver, these love tokens tapped directly into the romantic and sensitive side of people's nature and revived the passion for flowers and messages in jewellery last seen in the early 19th century. Thus the addition of an ivy leaf would signify friendship and forget-me-not true love. All kinds of everyday objects suddenly took on a new meaning when fashioned into little brooches – horseshoes, hearts, anchors and crosses were pumped out for an insatiably sentimental

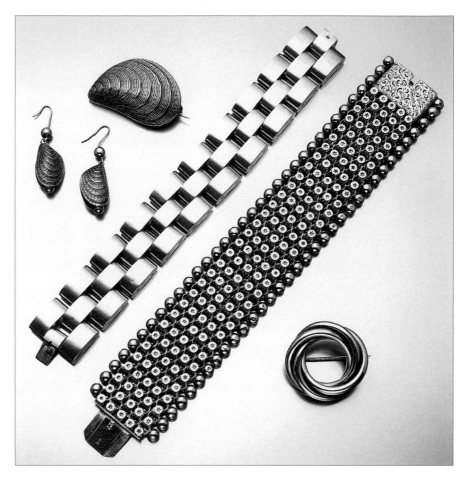

(Right) Group of silver bracelets and brooches c.1880.
Brian and Lynn Holmes; Pat Novissimo

(Below) Silver acorn brooch and earrings c.1885. Such 'figurative' jewellery was invariably hollow and is often dented or split down the seams.

and downright mawkish public, whilst patriotism was proudly observed in colourful flag pins and nationalistic symbols such as shamrocks and thistles.

Another extremely popular example of silver jewellery was the name brooch providing us with an ideal method of learning which girls' names were in common use at the end of the 19th century. Manufactured for working class women, these brooches were applied with block capitals spelling names such as Hilda, Ada, Florrie and Gladys in chiselled frames decorated with flowers and scrolls. Often bought by soldiers and sailors anxious to convey their affections to the sweetheart they were leaving behind, it is interesting to note that brooches depicting male names are practically non-existent. The sweetheart token with possibly the purest sentimental message was the Mizpah brooch. Taken from the Old Testament book of Genesis, Mizpah bade the Lord to 'watch over me and thee when we are parted from one another'.

The final group of silver brooches which has experienced a sharp rise in value is that with novelty and sporting designs. The Victorians were as

A range of silver sentimental 'sweetheart' brooches c.1880-1900. These are fascinating since they tell us the names which were in common usage at the end of the Victorian era. Other examples were overlaid in gold or depicted 'lucky' symbols such as horseshoes and shamrocks. Sylvie Spectrum

passionate about sport as we are today and brooches fashioned as tennis racquets (perhaps with the addition of a little silver ball), a pair of golf clubs, a cricket bat or boxing gloves are keenly sought – especially if the setting is engraved with the name of a sports association or prize winner. Bicycles with 'revolving' wheels are particularly collectable, as are novelties such as locomotives, ships and vintage cars. These evocative brooches were sometimes decorated with spots of enamel to highlight a funnel or carriage light, factors which can significantly heighten interest and corresponding value.

Further reading

Victorian Jewelry – Unexplored Treasures by Ginny Redington Dawes and Corinne Davidov (Abbeville Press)
Antique and 20th Century Jewellery by Vivienne Becker (NAG Press)

A silver belt buckle in the form of a bat by M. Erhart, 1908, a French silver dragon brooch, a Lalique silver coiled serpent brooch and a German silver gilt grotesque mask pendant, all c.1900. John Jesse

CHAPTER 16
ARTS AND CRAFTS AND ART NOUVEAU

ARTS AND CRAFTS

To attempt to put into perspective the mood which captured Britain around one hundred years ago for hand-made, artistically decorated gold and silverware, it may be helpful to inspect a reasonable jewellery auction taking place today. Together with the usual assortment of contemporary manufactured jewels, wristwatches and accessories will no doubt feature a cross-section of late Victorian and Edwardian rings, brooches, pendants and chains – certainly pretty and wearable, but often repetitive in design and lacking in artistic inspiration. To put it another way, one diamond half hoop ring or crescent brooch can look very much like another, while mass-produced silver bangles, engraved lockets, safety bar fasteners and gem pendants can be disappointingly unimaginative.

The Arts and Crafts Movement evolved as a direct backlash to the tidal wave of mechanical, industrialised output which engulfed Britain in the 1880s and 1890s. The problem was not only confined to the cheap end of the market since the discovery of the South African diamond fields served to flood jewellery shops with unexceptional and over duplicated designs for a wealthier clientele. It soon became apparent that much of this produce was ill-conceived, lacked artistic integrity and had 'lost its way' in the drive for commercial gain and profit.

Artistic jewellery had existed on the market since the 1850s, largely inspired by influential commentators such as John Ruskin and William Morris who, for example, deplored the sort of over-decorated and seemingly insensitive designs on show at the Great Exhibition of 1851. By the late 1880s several Guilds and Art Schools were founded upon socialist principles to promote a better understanding of decorative arts and to teach the theory and practical application of techniques such as enamelling, engraving, silversmithing and metal-working. In 1890 the Birmingham Guild of Handicraft was established and very soon numerous groups of artisans and students began to set up small workshops all over the country in which individual skills could be encouraged and perfected in an atmosphere of creative artistic harmony.

Adhering closely to idealistic principles, the sort of materials commonly used in Arts and Crafts jewellery were simple, understated, invariably inexpensive and lacked the flashy 'shallowness' of many precious gems. This was also a case of financial necessity, since many workers quite simply could not afford to use diamonds and gold in their designs. The primary metal was silver, sometimes decorated with strips of gold wire, while preferred gemstones included pearl, garnet, moonstone, turquoise, rock crystal, opal and amethyst. Hardstones were extensively used in all manner of buckles, necklaces and pendants, invariably polished 'en cabochon.' Among many varieties and colours, the most popular included royal blue lapis lazuli, bright green chrysoprase, onyx and sardonyx, cornelian and chalcedony. Enamel was the perfect substitute for gems and much Arts and Crafts jewellery is beautifully enhanced with translucent

Arts & Crafts silver and harlequin opal butterfly brooch c.1905.
Woolley & Wallis

141

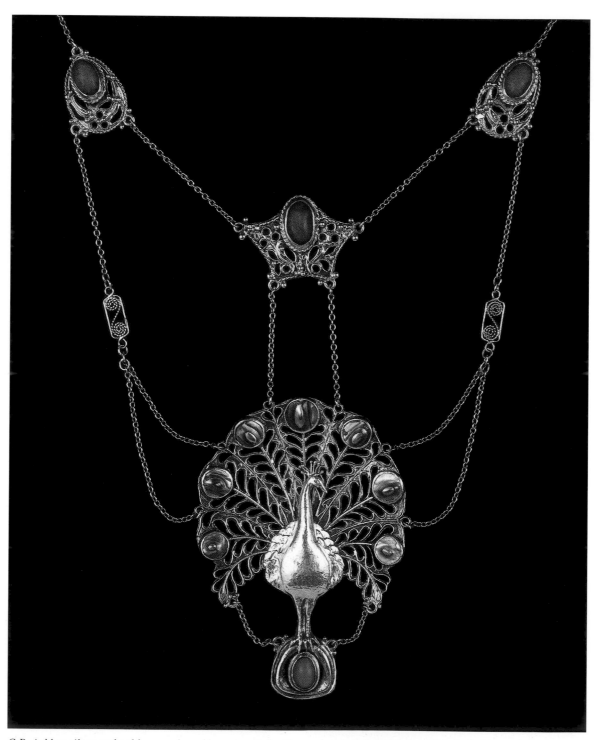

C.R. Ashbee silver and gold peacock necklace mounted with coral and abalone shell c.1900. Probably made by the Guild of Handicraft.

John Jesse

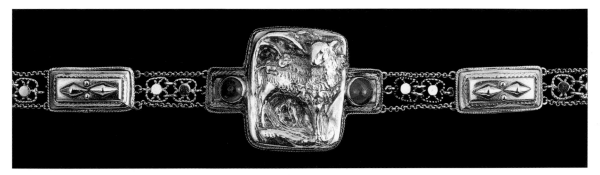

Henry Wilson Arts & Crafts silver bracelet, the central plaque embossed with a lamb flanked by two sapphire cabochons, c.1905.　　　　　　　　　　　　　　John Jesse

polychrome enamel decoration, sometimes in subtle merging shades and tones of which blues and greens were particularly favoured.

Undoubtedly, the most celebrated and influential coalescence of artists and artisans was the Guild of Handicraft, established in 1888 by Charles Robert Ashbee (1863-1942). Idealist, teacher and mentor to scores of artisans and designers, Ashbee never compromised his artistic principles – a factor which ultimately led to a serious falling out with 'commercial' entities, most notably Liberty & Co. Initially situated in London's East End, the Guild subsequently located in 1902 to Chipping Campden in Gloucestershire – a move which ultimately led to its decline and closure in 1908. As popular and appreciated as Arts and Crafts jewellery may be today, it also needs to be seen in the context of the time when much of the output was seen to be crude, primitive and artistically naïve.

Several designers certainly enjoyed a measure of success in their own lifetimes. Henry Wilson (1864-1934) trained as an architect before setting up a workshop in Kent. Inspired by medieval, Renaissance and Church symbolism, he produced important gold and silver jewellery and objects incorporating hardstones and gems decorated with powerful polychrome enamelling. Wilson employed

a team of young assistants who were encouraged to learn the essential techniques of metalwork, enamelling, engraving and the setting of stones.

John Paul Cooper (1869-1933) and Henry George Murphy (1884-1939) eventually progressed to launch their own businesses in which the influence of their apprenticeship served under Wilson was clearly apparent. Both men designed highly proficient gold and silver jewellery set with colourful gems

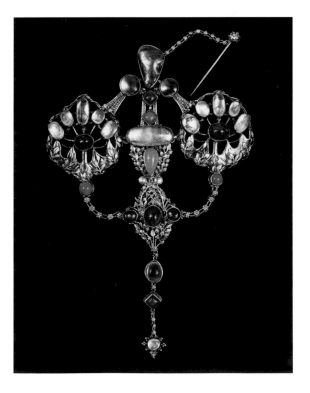

Gold corsage brooch by John Paul Cooper c.1908. Like Murphy, J.P. Cooper served his apprenticeship under Henry Wilson and the influence of his teacher and mentor are plainly visible.　　　　　　　John Jesse

(Above) Sapphire cabochon, enamel and gem-set gold pendant and chain by H.G. Murphy c.1890. Murphy, who served his apprenticeship under Henry Wilson, was an extraordinarily versatile designer craftsman whose output embraced such diverse themes as ecclesiastical silver and Art Deco diamonds.   Private Collection

(Above right) The back of the same jewel exhibiting Murphy's minute attention to detail.

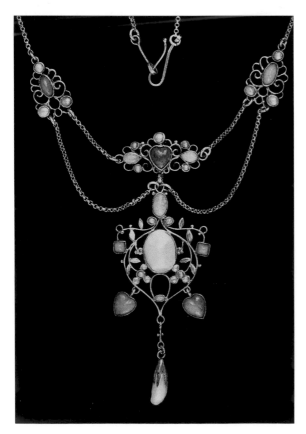

such as star ruby, sapphire and moonstone. Murphy in particular specialised in champlevé enamelling in settings which extended effortlessly in their range from the Gothic to the Renaissance and even the Orient.

Phoebe Traquair (1852-1936) was an Edinburgh artist who specialised in iridescent enamels embellished with highlights of gold in naturalistic gold frames which were sometimes suspended below iridescent 'gemstones' of foil-backed glass. The technique of using metallic foil to accentuate a design was first pioneered by Alexander Fisher (1864-1936), formerly a partner of Henry Wilson. Fisher was a highly influential teacher of the art of medieval and later enamelling and his work exhibits a strong influence of early designs from Limoges in France.

Arthur and Georgina Gaskin (1862-1928 and 1868-1934) met while students at the Birmingham School of Art. After marrying, they began to design jewellery distinctive for its extraordinary detail of

Silver necklace by Arthur and Georgina Gaskin mounted with pearls, opals, mother-of-pearl and pale green chrysoprase cabochons c.1905.   John Jesse

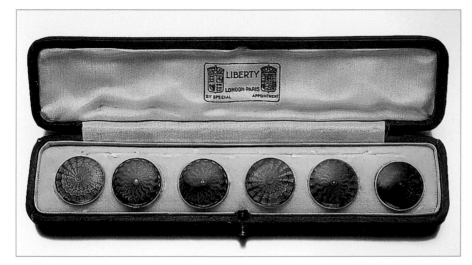

Set of six Liberty translucent enamel buttons c.1905. These pretty buttons are visibly enhanced in value by being in their original Liberty box.
Shapiro & Co

densely clustered leaves, flowers and naturalistic motifs enamelled in bright pastel colours such as pink, blue and green and embellished with pearls and mother-of-pearl plaques.

Those designers willing to allow their jewellery and silverware to be exposed in the commercial sector found the ideal venue for their talents at the London premises established by Arthur Lazenby Liberty (1843-1917). Liberty & Co initially specialised in selling Oriental textiles and works of art before its founder turned to commissioning contemporary metalwork from a group of influential Arts and Crafts designers such as Christopher Dresser, Bernard Cuzner, the Gaskins and Jessie M. King, a student of the Glasgow School of Art celebrated for enamelled jewels, accessories and fabrics.

Probably the best known of all Liberty's craftsmen was Archibald Knox (1864-1933), an extraordinarily versatile goldsmith, silversmith and metalworker equally adept in the production of small-scale gem-set pendants or massive bowls decorated with enamel. Knox was chief designer of Liberty's *Cymric* range of silver goods based upon Celtic themes. Jewellery such as brooches, buckles and pendants were strongly organic in inspiration, often

Liberty & Co turquoise and gold pendant probably designed by Archibald Knox c.1905.

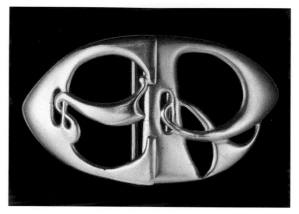

This buckle exhibits the characteristic Knox 'whiplash' motif. A subtle representation of the monogram ER, it was designed to commemorate the Coronation of Edward VII in 1901.   John Jesse

Definitive Archibald Knox. A gold, mother-of-pearl and Mississippi pearl pendant with twist link chain threaded with freshwater pearls. Designed by Knox for Liberty & Co., c.1900.   John Jesse

exhibiting Knox's characteristic 'whiplash' motifs, while enamels in subtle shades of blue and green were particularly favoured.

Omar Ramsden (1873-1939) and Alwyn Carr (1872-1940) met while students at the Sheffield School of Art and subsequently formed a partnership based in London from 1898 to 1919 where they produced a wide range of jewellery, silverware and ceremonial pieces of medieval inspiration.

Murrle Bennett & Co was a competitor to Liberty founded in 1884 and owned by Ernest Murrle, a German who settled in London. Much of the firm's output was similar to the Liberty Cymric range; indeed, Murrle Bennett even sold goods to their rivals. Jewellery designs included gold pendants, brooches and bracelets which were often mounted with blister pearls and turquoises polished 'en cabochon' or left in their native matrix.

Child & Child, a London shop owned by Walter and Harold Child, specialised in Arts and Crafts silver jewellery such as buckles and hatpins which were enamelled in striking shades of metallic blue and green on a guilloché field. The firm also experimented with plique-à-jour enamel; much of

'Gothic' silver and enamel locket pendant and chain by Omar Ramsden depicting St George in an appropriately heroic stance, c.1905.   John Jesse

Silver and enamel pendant by Charles Horner c.1910. Based in Halifax, Charles Horner mass-produced functional and affordable silver jewellery such as hatpins, pendants and simple brooches with enamel decoration.
RBR Group at Grays

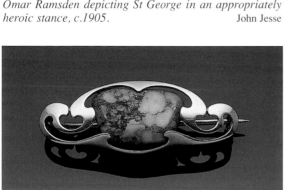

Gold brooch by Murrle Bennett mounted with a turquoise matrix pebble c.1900.   Shapiro & Co

their output was sold in their characteristic bright green leather boxes.

Charles Horner was a Halifax firm which produced very large quantities of silver accessories such as hatpins as well as inexpensive brooches and pendants containing enamel, small pearls and gems.

Finally, Sibyl Dunlop (1889-1968), while not strictly speaking a competitor of Liberty, established a retail shop in Kensington Church Street with a

(Left) Gold and silver roundel brooch and earclips set with water sapphires and assorted gems by Sibyl Dunlop. John Jesse

(Below) Silver and multi gem-set clip by Dorrie Nossiter c.1910. Dorrie Nossiter's colourful jewellery was rarely, if ever, signed and her work is regularly confused with Sibyl Dunlop. Here the original box confirms origin definitively.
Mrs Etienne Brown

team of craftsmen specialising in bold silver jewels set with clusters of multi-colour gemstones and pearls which were further decorated with leaves and scrolls of gold.

Arts and Crafts in Europe

The impact of the Arts and Crafts movement was felt throughout Europe and Scandinavia, even extending to America where firms such as Tiffany & Co produced exotic jewellery using a range of new and innovative materials. Art Nouveau in Germany was known as 'Jugendstil' ('Youth Style') and drew heavily on both the rich symbolism of nature fundamental to the Arts and Crafts movement and the strong linear forms of 1930s Art Deco.

Theodor Fahrner (1859-1919) was a German manufacturer of 'affordable art jewellery' who initially collaborated with Murrle Bennett in the manufacture of elegant, naturalistic silver and enamel brooches and pendants and then switched production towards functional, architectural themes set with marcasite and bold hardstone combinations such as coral and onyx. The Darmstadt Colony was a community of artists and designers located at Pforzheim while in Austria the Wiener Werkstatte (Vienna Workshop) largely drew inspiration from the English Guild of Handicraft.

The Danish silversmith Georg Jensen (1866-1935) founded a workshop in Copenhagen in association

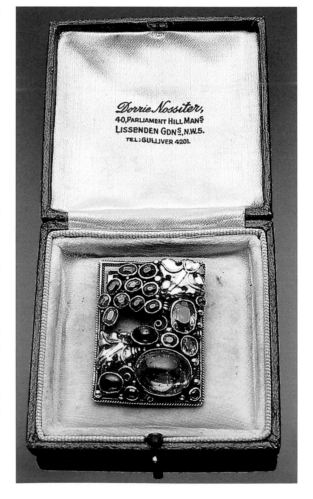

Group of Georg Jensen silver jewellery, early to mid-20th century.
Sylvie Spectrum

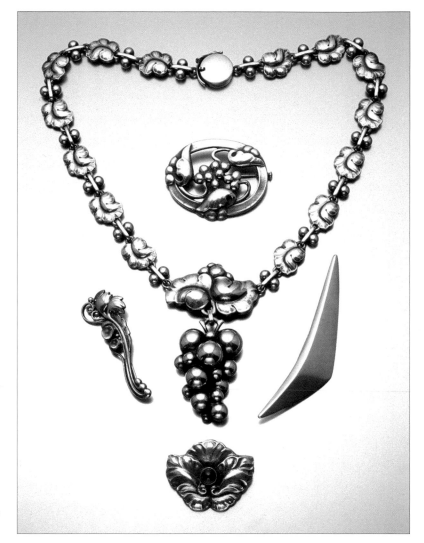

Silver, opal, enamel and gold 'Jugendstil' brooch by Theodor Fahrner exhibiting the plain linear form characteristic of German Art Nouveau. John Jesse

with Mogens Ballin (1871-1914). Adopting a range of themes including flowers, birds and leaves, Jensen specialised in the use of polished hardstone cabochons – moonstone, lapis lazuli and garnet – in bold silver figurative settings which make as great an impact today as they did in the early 1900s.

ART NOUVEAU

Chronologically Arts and Crafts and Art Nouveau ran side by side and stylistically there are several clear comparisons to be drawn: the overwhelming influence of nature; organic imagery in which the cold, mechanical forms of late 19th century mass-produced adornment were totally shunned; the abundant use of enamel and particular gems selected for their aesthetic beauty such as pearl, opal, moonstone and turquoise.

Of the differences, the most obvious was the overwhelming impression of sensuousness and nature running riot, where enamel flowers or jewelled insects and serpents were woven into exotic armlets or stunning hair combs. As well as the modest, understated hardstone cabochons of the standard Arts and Crafts ornament, the Art Nouveau equivalent was

the naturalistic ideal or accentuate fantastic, dream-like symbolism.

The term 'Art Nouveau' was taken from a Parisian shop called 'Maison de L'Art Nouveau' which was owned by an influential entrepreneur, Samuel Bing. The period in which the movement flourished was the last decade of the 19th century until the outbreak of the First World War. During these twenty-five years, Art Nouveau gained enormous influence in France, Belgium, Italy, Spain and America, the latter in no small part due to the great commercial success of Tiffany & Co.

Whilst nature and naturalism was the driving force behind nearly all the decorative output, there was an altogether darker side to many of the jewellery designs. A sensuous female form would bear the torso of an insect such as a moth or dragonfly with folded enamel wings. A bouquet of flowers would, on closer inspection, be in a transitional state of decay. This representation of the cycle of nature was brilliantly articulated by René Lalique (1860-1945), whose jewellery combined a number of distinct features which set his work apart from the vast majority of his contemporaries. Lalique possessed an extraordinarily fertile imagination. Once he had carefully studied the natural form in its own habitat – perhaps an insect such as a butterfly, a bird, a flower or a leaf – he would then interpret its essential

frequently mounted in gold and set with valuable precious stones such as emerald, ruby, sapphire and, notably, diamond – as a decorative embellishment or even the focal point of the complete jewel. Innovative and breathtaking 'new' materials typified the Art Nouveau period and ground-breaking designer goldsmiths such as René Lalique pioneered the application of daring organic media such as horn or artificial materials like moulded glass to reinforce

Two dragonfly brooches. The lower example is French c.1900 set with diamonds, ruby and opalescent enamel wings. The upper brooch is a modern reproduction highlighted by the rather 'hard' plique-à-jour enamel wings. Bentley & Skinner

Quintessential Art Nouveau jewel by René Lalique. The etched contours and subtle definition of the hardstone evoke an almost fairy-tale quality to this lovely study which could have been lifted directly from the pages of A Midsummer Night's Dream.

(Above) A superb Art Nouveau opal, diamond, ruby and demantoid garnet brooch by Maison Vever c.1905.   S.J. Phillips

(Right) Symbolist jewel in plique-à-jour, ivory, emerald and diamond by Philippe Wolfers, a Belgian goldsmith celebrated for imaginative designs combining diverse naturalistic themes.

characteristics into a spectacular pendant, comb or buckle startling in originality and technically incomparable, observing the minutest attention to detail in the setting and the materials. Plique-à-jour enamel was a particularly favoured medium, thus the wings of a dragonfly would contain a network of gauze-like *cloisons* or cells which were individually filled with a series of translucent glass panels in several subtle colours. Organic materials such as horn were reserved for hair combs which were sometimes stained or applied with compatible gems such as moonstones to suggest raindrops.

The human form was a popular and potent symbol for many Art Nouveau goldsmiths. The House of Vever was a dynasty of French jewellers which produced splendid botanical jewels sometimes incorporating the profile of a maiden in moulded glass. Vever designs are somewhat more reserved than Lalique's essentially flamboyant style and the settings are decidedly linear.

Philippe Wolfers (1858-1929) was a Belgian who designed a limited range of strangely evocative enamel and gem-set brooches and pendants incorporating the figure of a maiden in carved ivory. Lucien Gaillard often worked with horn, designing elegant combs of floral inspiration bearing a strong Japanese influence, while Alphonse Fouquet (1828-1911) and his son Georges (1862-1957) changed direction from the production of highly coloured Neo-Renaissance jewellery to flamboyant and exotic

Unusual carved horn hair comb by Georges Fouquet decorated with enamel and opals. The design is strongly Egyptian in influence, c.1908. John Jesse

French carved horn and glass bead pendant on cordette by Bonté c.1905. John Jesse

avant-garde designs for theatrical figureheads such as Alphonse Mucha.

It has to be said that jewels by Wolfers, Fouquet and their contemporaries are, today, extremely rare and desperately expensive. Examples in pristine condition will easily fetch high five figure prices while an important piece by René Lalique can achieve over £100,000. Nevertheless, inexpensive and pretty Art Nouveau jewellery does appear fairly regularly in the specialist retail and auction sectors, especially enamelled brooches, pendants, rings and accessories. Modest, unsigned and unattributed French gold brooches, silver pendants or horn hair combs can still be bought for less than £1,000, although the addition of a few precious gems, pearls or plique-à-jour enamel will raise prices visibly. Condition is vital since the loss of enamel or a later repair is very difficult to rectify. Finally, do ensure that a piece which bears the label 'Art Nouveau' is genuine since large numbers of modern repro-ductions such as silver 'dragonfly' brooches, sets of buttons and photograph frames regularly appear at auction bearing rather 'non-committal' descriptions which mask their dubious origin.

Further reading

Pre-Raphaelite to Arts and Crafts Jewellery by Charlotte Gere and Geoffrey Munn (Antique Collectors' Club)

Jewelry & Metalwork in the Arts and Crafts Tradition by Elyse Zorn Karlin (Schiffer Publishing Ltd.)

Art Nouveau Jewellery by Vivienne Becker (E.P. Dutton)

CHAPTER 17

THE BELLE ÉPOQUE: EARLY PLATINUM JEWELLERY AND THE 'GARLAND' STYLE

The restless, ever-changing profile of jewellery design in the 20th century was strongly influenced by the complex array of social, economic and artistic influences which characterised this turbulent era. Until the First World War several contrasting decorative themes ran concurrently and it was perfectly possible to find one jeweller selling a traditional stock of reliable but conservative diamond jewels – formal tiaras, star brooches and half hoop bangles – while his neighbour would specialise in the bold, daring themes of the Art Nouveau movement – brightly coloured enamel buckles, serpent bracelets and woodland diadems.

The term which was adopted to embrace the lighter, feminine designs of the Edwardian era in yet another contrasting expression of the craftsman's art was *Belle Époque*. Designers turned away from the heavy and predictable look of the Victorian era and

(Above) A good example of a turn of the 20th century transitional brooch exhibiting Victorian features (the bow surmount and gold claw setting of the sapphire) and Edwardian characteristics (the diamond wreath and platinum claws).

(Left) Splendid platinum sapphire and diamond bow brooch with multiple swags, drops and Garland style leaf decoration c.1905. A veritable tour de force of Belle Epoque corsage jewellery.   Hancocks & Co

Pair of platinum and diamond earrings c.1910 mounted with moulded black glass plaques depicting neo-classical 'putti' subjects. Woolley & Wallis

Platinum, pearl and diamond pendant c.1905 with characteristic millegrain bead edging to the lines of diamonds.

Belle Epoque platinum, aquamarine, pearl and diamond brooch in the Garland style c.1905-1910.

began to create altogether lighter and more elegant pieces which were clearly inspired by the delicate imagery of French rococo decoration from the end of the 18th century. Thus pretty shell and lattice motifs, swags, bows and hearts were seamlessly combined with charming naturalistic symbols such as sprays of leaves, flowerheads and trails of tendrils in a range of wonderfully feminine jewellery known as the *Garland Style*.

As technically adept as craftsmen were during this period, such fine and intricate workmanship would have been impossible to achieve without the

Delicate Belle Epoque platinum and diamond bracelet in the 'Garland' style c.1905.   Woolley & Wallis

introduction of platinum, a brand new metal which both revolutionised jewellery design and irrevocably changed how diamonds and gems were fashioned and retained within their settings. Unlike silver, platinum is substantially harder and stronger. This meant that precious stones, and diamonds in particular, could be mounted in unobtrusive claws or gripped in minute beaded lines and clusters known as *millegrain* settings. Platinum was therefore an ideal vehicle for 'Garland' jewellery in which tiny diamonds were placed into complex sprays of leaves or set in articulated swags, drops and latticework clusters.

The first quarter of the 20th century also saw significant advances in diamond cutting and polishing. The standard cut of the Victorian era was the old European brilliant – usually cushion in shape and with a tendency towards being thick and ill-proportioned. By the First World War several new and innovative cuts began to appear in English, French and Continental diamond jewellery including the marquise, the pendeloque, the lunette (half moon) and, of course, the round brilliant. Better proportions meant altogether more 'life' and 'sparkle'. Many diamonds used by prominent jewellers in the Belle Époque era were of a superior colour and clarity, another reason why early platinum jewellery is so highly sought today.

As well as fancy shaped diamonds, coloured gems also began to be used far more extensively. Fine rubies from Burma, emeralds from Colombia and sapphires from Burma and Kashmir accompanied diamonds in a broad range of formal and everyday

Boucheron gem-set lapel watch with painted study of putti in a landscape.
Bentley & Skinner

Delicate platinum and diamond articulated pendant. By around 1910 diamond cutting had progressed to the extent that fancy shapes such as pears, marquises and hearts were available on the market, leading to a complete reassessment of how jewellery could be constructed and worn.
Woolley & Wallis

155

Pair of platinum, emerald, diamond and emerald bead earrings c.1915. The emerald drops at the bottom are probably from an antique Indian jewel such as a Sarpech. The remounting of Mughal and later Indian gems was a feature of Cartier and other French jewellers in the 1920s and 1930s. Woolley & Wallis

designs ranging from elaborate collars and corsage ornaments to simple pendants and earrings.

Of all so-called 'precious' gems, the 'species' which is most closely associated with *garland* jewellery is the pearl. Subtle and understated, the neutral off-white, cream, pink and golden tones of this most elegant of gems perfectly complemented the flashy brilliance of diamonds. These were the days before cultured pearls irrevocably changed the industry. All the pearls used were of natural origin and thus highly prized for their beauty and rarity. Invariably smooth in lustre and found in a variety of interesting shapes such as compressed boutons,

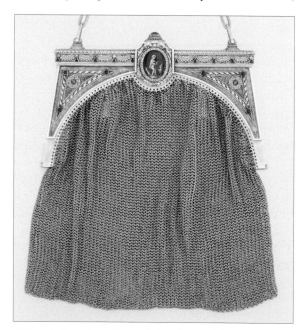

(Above) French gold mesh handbag with neo-classical frame decorated with pastel enamels, gems and a Limoges enamel plaque of a cherub c.1905.

(Left) Multi-row seed pearl rope pattern sautoir necklace with tassel pendant c.1910. The tassel cap is diamond-set and suspends polished sapphire pipkin drops. Even the bolt ring above the tassel is diamond-set. Hancocks & Co

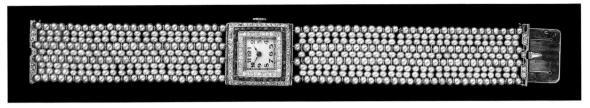

(Above) Multi-row pearl mesh bracelet watch with sapphire and diamond case c.1915. Hancocks & Co

(Left) Pair of millegrain-set diamond cluster earrings c.1910. Woolley & Wallis

Cartier Oriental pearl and diamond hexafoil pendant in platinum c.1910. Hancocks & Co

teardrops and strange baroque forms rather like bunches of grapes, pearls could be adapted into any number of designs. One of the most popular of these was the *sautoir,* a long necklace of interwoven seed pearl strands with tassel finials in pretty diamond and gem-set cap settings.

Rings conformed closely to the Belle Époque ideal. Pretty and understated, gems and diamonds were millegrain-set in target clusters, bows and hearts whilst their platinum mounts were further embellished with reeded decoration, engraved scrolls and even tiny rose diamonds in their galleries. Pendants and earrings were invariably composed of a round brilliant-cut diamond top stone supporting a larger pear-shaped diamond, Oriental pearl or precious stone drop. Designs were thus extremely simple but highly effective. The *negligée* pendant is typical of this genre where two gems are connected by either a platinum or white gold rod and worn suspended from a simple matching trace chain. Brooches could range from the most basic bars set with a single stone or series of graduated gems to far more elaborate geometric shapes – roundels, squares, ovals and fans – in which the diamond frames are pierced with a delicate tracery to suggest gauze-like mesh, honeycombs and cobwebs. These superb brooches and pendants really were the finest examples of the craftsman's art since the mounts were sometimes composed of a series of tiny joints

enabling the articulated jewel to be literally rolled or folded in half.

The demand for fine Belle Époque, Edwardian and early platinum jewellery has, frankly, never been higher and prime pieces, especially of French manufacture, will achieve top prices at auction or in the retail sector. Nevertheless, simple 'Garland' diamond pieces can still be bought relatively cheaply while secondary jewellery such as gold negligée pendants set with semi-precious stones, half pearl latticework brooches and simple diamond or gem-set bar brooches are still highly affordable and can make just as big an impact as costly 'formal' examples.

Further reading

Understanding Jewellery by David Bennett and Daniela Mascetti (Antique Collectors' Club)

Jewelry from Antiquity to the Present by Clare Phillips (Thames & Hudson)

Cartier 1900-1939 by Judy Rudoe (British Museum Press)

CHAPTER 18
FABERGÉ, TIFFANY, CARTIER AND THEIR CONTEMPORARIES

Why buy signed jewellery?

There is absolutely no doubt that a signature on a piece of well-made jewellery will enhance its value. In the case of some half a dozen celebrated international houses, this added premium can be quite considerable.

Manufacturers of luxury goods in general have always traded on the caché of their name and reputation. In some disciplines the difference in quality between the established product and its unattributed imitator can be purely negligible, demonstrating over and over again that a 'good name' conveys reassurance, style, social acceptability and old-fashioned snob appeal.

In the 19th century revivalist goldsmiths such as Castellani, Giuliano and Brogden routinely signed their jewellery with a house monogram. By the early

(Above) Boucheron French emerald and diamond bracelet c.1925. The emeralds are probably of Indian Mughal origin.
Hancocks & Co

(Top) Boucheron diamond tambourine brooch with enamelled troubadour motif c.1900. This rare and unusual jewel is further decorated with diamond rondels (flat, faceted discs) around the frame.
Sandra Cronan

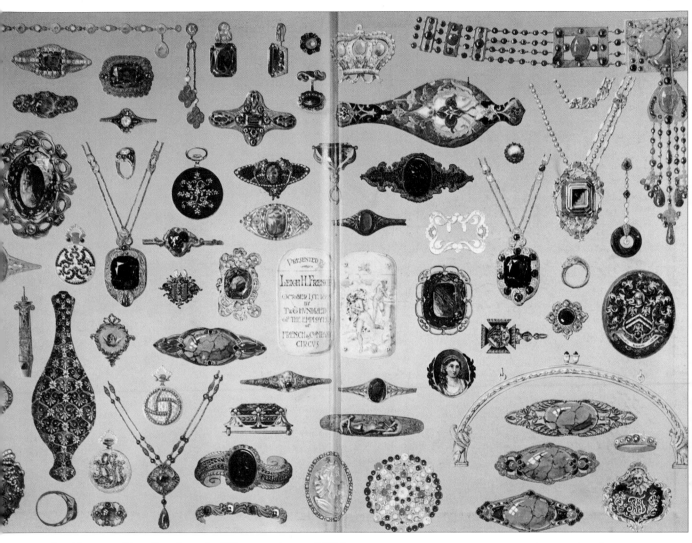

Double page of jewellery from the Tiffany catalogue of 1890.   Tiffany & Co./Bridgeman Art Library

20th century Parisian jewellers such as Cartier, Boucheron and Chaumet not only signed their creations but engraved a unique serial number on the mount to prove authenticity and provide a 'library record' of the item's existence. Unfortunately, in a world fixated by good provenance, the evidence of a signature has given rise to the continuing and growing problem of fakes in which the addition of a spurious name can dramatically increase value. The

problem is most deep rooted and widespread in the field of Fabergé where the sheer number of fakes on the market, occasionally proficient and frequently dreadful, have resulted in an ironic term being coined in the Fine Art lexicon – Fauxbergé.

So, why buy a clip by Cartier or bangle by Bulgari? The answer, quite simply, is reliability and superior craftsmanship. Raw materials such as diamonds, precious stones and their accompanying settings are

Fabergé diamond-set tiara c.1900 inspired by the crown made for Catherine the Great by Jacob and Jean-François André Duval in 1801.   Wartski Ltd.

carefully selected for their quality and consistency. Designs are bold, imaginative, exciting, thoroughly wearable and – a key asset in the world of jewellery – invariably timeless. Signed jewellery tends to be that much more expensive but the long term commercial benefits may be considerable.

Fabergé Siberian topaz and diamond brooch in the neo-classical taste c.1900 in the original fitted hollywood box.

Fabergé translucent lilac guilloché enamel, gold and diamond-set photograph frame. Fabergé frames often appear in interesting geometric shapes such as diamonds and six-pointed stars; the back covers are invariably cut from a sheet of ivory. Workmaster Michael Perchin, St Petersburg 1890-1895. Woolley & Wallis

Peter Carl Fabergé

The life of this extraordinary goldsmith is well documented. Born on 30 May 1846, he attended business school in Dresden and subsequently visited Paris where he was heavily influenced by the abundance of neo-classical art and architecture on display in the Louvre. At the age of twenty-four he took over control of his father's shop in St Petersburg and quickly gained a reputation for designing jewellery, silver and objets d'art of unparalleled elegance and originality. In 1884 he was commissioned by Tsar Alexander III to make the first Imperial

Easter egg. This set the seal on a unique relationship between Fabergé and the Romanovs which was to continue right up to the cataclysmic events of the Bolshevik revolution in 1917. Indeed, Fabergé was fortunate to escape from Russia as a courier attached to the British Embassy. He died in Lausanne on 24 September 1920.

Fabergé's astonishing success was founded upon several critical factors. He was a brilliant marketing strategist and his relationship with the Imperial family opened many doors of influence throughout Europe. Perhaps his greatest success was expanding

Russian four leaf clover brooch c.1895-1900 together with a pair of Fabergé Siberian jade, ruby and diamond cufflinks c.1900-1910.

A group of Fabergé hardstone, enamel and jewelled egg pendants. Still fairly common today, miniature eggs offer collectors an accessible method of buying Russian jewellery at reasonable prices.　Bentley & Skinner

production to include purely decorative objets d'art – his so-called 'Objects of Fantasy' such as hardstone carvings, flower studies, toys and the celebrated Imperial Easter eggs. He made extensive use of translucent enamel recognising the importance of a medium which could decorate a large surface area and which often took the place of costly gemstones. He also perfected the technique of using several different colours of gold in his settings and favoured gems and hardstones which were indigenous to Russia such as Siberian jade, rhodonite and lapis lazuli. Even the wood used in photograph frames and jewellery boxes was of Russian origin – palisander, Karelian birch and

pale brown hollywood.

Much of the Fabergé sold today fetches colossal sums at international auction. Nevertheless, it is still possible to buy modest brooches, small items of jewellery such as tiepins, cufflinks and miniature egg pendants in the salerooms, although condition is a crucial factor. Fakes can be difficult to spot, however. As a general guideline, look out for garish enamel colours which contain bubbles when examined under a lens, crude settings to gems, poor quality goldwork and – a useful indicator for copies – makers' marks and assay stamps which are too obvious, too 'crisp' and too plentiful.

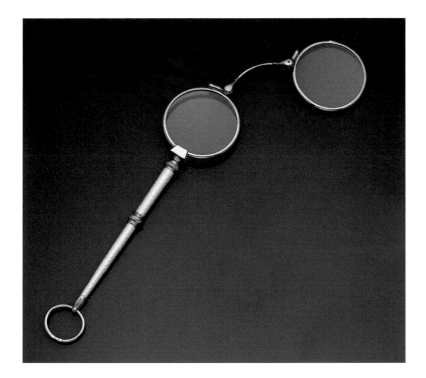

(Left) Pair of Fabergé deux couleur *gold lorgnettes enamelled in oyster white, workmaster Henrik Wigstrom c.1900.* Woolley & Wallis

(Below) Tiffany & Co. diamond chrysanthemum brooch with a cluster of Mississippi pearl petals c.1910. Wartski Ltd.

Tiffany and Jewellery in America

Extraordinarily versatile and original, Tiffany & Co are rightly regarded as the leading pioneers of American jewellery and decorative arts since the 19th century. The firm was established by Charles Lewis Tiffany (1812-1902) in New York, initially specialising in giftware and stationery. The stock was gradually expanded to include jewellery imported from Paris. The success of this operation led the firm to start designing and making its own distinctive jewels which, by the early 1900s, embraced a number of contrasting themes from traditional diamond and precious stone pieces in the fashionable 'Garland' style to bold and vibrant Art Nouveau floral studies and colourful enamelled symbolist jewellery mounted with unusual gemstones such as harlequin opal, fire opal and Montana sapphire.

On the death of C.L. Tiffany in 1902 the business was taken over by his son, Louis Comfort Tiffany (1848-1933), who developed many aspects of the decorative arts for which the company is celebrated today, most notably studio lamps, 'favrile' glass, ceramics, silver and metalware. In the 1950s several young and innovative craftsmen were commissioned to design their own jewellery for the company of which the most prominent was Jean Schlumberger, a Frenchman who introduced a range of chunky,

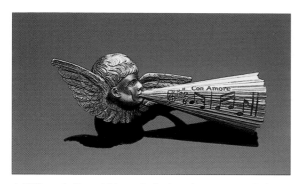 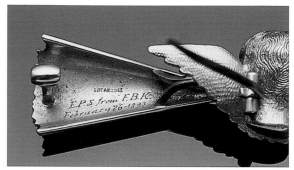

A Tiffany & Co gold brooch designed as a winged cherub blaring a stylised puff of wind enamelled with the motto 'con amore'. A highly personal and romantic jewel, the mount is signed and engraved 'February 26 1893'.

Mrs. Sylvia Quenet-Chute

Reverse of the Tiffany brooch illustrating the Tiffany signature.

enamelled gold bangles, earclips and rings exhibiting the famous Tiffany 'kiss' motif. This concept of independent artists developing their own range of ideas has continued right up to the present day with attractive and wearable jewellery designed by Paloma Picasso and Elsa Peretti now sold in Tiffany shops all over the world.

Tiffany is one of a group of prominent jewellers active in America from the early 1900s. Several of these long established firms, such as Oscar Heyman and Seaman Schepps of New York, are flourishing today. Each developed their own distinctive house style with the added ingredient of American flair and originality. Black, Starr and Frost produced elegant diamond jewellery in the European taste as far back as the 1850s, while another firm, J.E. Caldwell of Philadelphia, designed particularly pretty 'Belle Époque' platinum and gem-set pieces prized for their technical virtuosity.

The New York firm Marcus & Co is closely associated with Art Nouveau enamel gold work. Unlike its European contemporaries, however, it chose to use plique-à-jour enamel in striking, dominant colours. This sense of confidence extended to its collection of Art Deco diamond jewellery which reflected the mood of innovation and flair in America between the wars.

Cartier, Van Cleef & Arpels and Boucheron
The progress of international jewellery from the end of the 19th century has, to quite a considerable extent, been driven by three Parisian firms which are recognised all over the world for the fantastic quality of their raw materials, their breathtaking imagination and the sheer brilliance of their designs. Each business has adapted its jewellery and accessories to keep ahead of the changing times and has pioneered advances in a broad range of skills from enamelling to the cutting and setting of gems. Ultimately all have played a major part in the way jewellery is worn today.

Cartier
The firm was founded in Paris in 1847 by Louis-François Cartier (1819-1904) and was subsequently taken over by his three grandsons Louis (1875-1942), Pierre (1878-1965) and Jacques (1884-1942) who each took responsibility for the development of the firm's operations in Paris, New York and London. The business was built up and consolidated by forging sound relationships with a host of important clients including European and international royalty, wealthy American financiers and industrialists, film stars and VIPs.

The great strength of Cartier was the firm's ability to introduce a wide and varied range of inspirations and themes into its jewellery designs, particularly during the years between the two world wars. Once Cartier had established itself as the leading manufacturer of jewellery in the 'Garland' style producing

Cartier Art Deco aquamarine and diamond clip brooch c.1935. Wartski Ltd.

Mughal gems were set in chic articulated Oriental diamond frames by the firm's Paris workshops, jewels in the Egyptian taste depicted pyramids, lotus flowers and 'Pharaonic' motifs fashioned from a combination of artfully set gems such as onyx, emerald and ruby, while Chinese and Japanese jewellery, clocks and accessories skilfully blended jet-black lacquer with a combination of coral, diamond and jade influenced by Oriental symbolism such as dragons, clouds and knotwork.

By the 1930s the taste for Art Deco 'architectural' jewellery was in full swing and Cartier adapted its designs once again to create a stunning range of bold and original jewels in which gems were purposely cut, shaped and set to reinforce the sense of geometry and linear structure fashionable at the time. During the 1940s and 1950s the firm introduced a series of striking gold jewels inspired by such diverse themes as 'bicycle chains' and 'gaspipes'. In the 1970s the firm's 'Must de Cartier' range was introduced to create a line of affordable and wearable jewellery, wristwatches and accessories; indeed Cartier wristwatches such as the 'Panthère', 'Tank Française' and 'Pasha' are among the most popular models available on the market today.

a constant flow of imposing diamond, platinum and pearl corsage ornaments, lavish collars, diadems and bandeaux, it turned its attention to exotic jewellery inspired by the art of Persia, Ancient Egypt, India, Russia and China. Thus fine old

Cartier platinum and diamond bracelet watch c.1930. Hancocks & Co

A fine quality Cartier onyx and diamond bracelet watch c.1925. The cover of the watch face has been cut from a solid diamond. Hancocks & Co

165

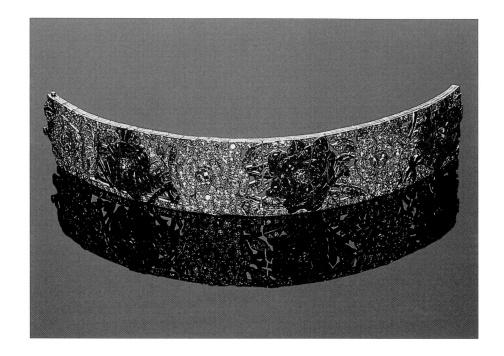

Van Cleef & Arpels

The firm was established in Paris in 1898 when Alfred Van Cleef (1873-1938) formed an association with his two brothers-in-law Charles Arpels (1880-1951) and Julien Arpels (1884-1964).

The technique with which Van Cleef & Arpels is most closely associated today is 'serti invisible' (invisible setting) in which rubies or sapphires are set in side-by-side formation with no apparent metal or mounting visible from the front. This sophisticated

(Top) Splendid Van Cleef & Arpels platinum, ruby, emerald, onyx and diamond bracelet c.1920-1925. The rubies are individually 'invisibly set' so no metal is visible between the actual gems. Such jewels fetch substantial sums at international auction.

(Left) Van Cleef & Arpels naturalistic platinum brooch in the japonaiserie taste. Made in 1927, this exquisite jewel is set with mirror-cut diamonds in the butterfly and individually polished and shaped emeralds and sapphires in the cornflower – elegance and technical virtuosity seamlessly combined. Woolley & Wallis

method involved chiselling grooves into the back of each individual stone and sliding them on to a series of gold or platinum rails. The technique made an enormous impact when it first appeared in 1935 and was used to great effect in brooches, bracelets and earclips of floral cluster and leaf design.

In the 1920s and 1930s the firm produced striking naturalistic and architectural jewels such as bracelets of 'Egyptian' influence inspired by the discovery of Tutankhamun's tomb in 1922 and, in the early 1940s, a range of distinctive broad gold bracelets and brooch clips composed of a series of honeycomb shaped sections known as 'ludo hexagone' motifs. Like their celebrated contemporary Cartier, Van Cleef & Arpels moved with the times and by the 1960s the firm began to create a range of strongly chromatic jewellery set with contrasting gems such as polished emerald and ruby cabochons and diamonds in yellow gold mounts.

Boucheron

After a fairly modest start at a small jewellery shop founded in 1858, Frédéric Boucheron (1830-1902) moved to far grander premises at 26 Place Vendôme, Paris. Much of Boucheron's early success was his reputation as a society jeweller supplying formal diamond jewels – tiaras, corsage brooches and elaborate collars – to brides, bridesmaids and their guests at formal wedding receptions held in the capital. Exactly like Cartier, Van Cleef & Arpels and other leading French jewellers such as Chaumet and Vever, Boucheron moved with the changing times and by the end of the 19th century was producing highly original pieces using innovative materials – for example, plique-à-jour enamel and gold combined with base metals. After Frédéric Boucheron died in 1902 the business was continued by his son Louis. In 1907 a shop was founded in London. Boucheron jewellery exhibits a distinctive style with a strong tendency towards formality, boldness and colour. Some of the firm's Art Deco jewellery – their range of carved hardstone flower jewellery, for instance – displays a marvellous imagination blended with exceptional technical skill.

A fine example of gold relief work in a Boucheron cigarette case. The various textures lend a three-dimensional quality to this Japanese landscape which is further embellished with precious gems, tortoiseshell and a delightful study of a swan in a lake of mother-of-pearl, c.1910-1915.

Further reading

Cartier by Hans Nadelhoffer (Thames & Hudson)

Cartier 1900-1939 by Judy Rudoe (British Museum Press)

The Art of Carl Fabergé by Kenneth Snowman (Faber & Faber)

Fabergé's Imperial Jewels by Géza von Habsburg and Marina Lopato (Fabergé Arts Foundation)

Jewelry in America by Martha Gandy Fales (Antique Collectors' Club)

CHAPTER 19
ART DECO AND THE ARCHITECTURAL REVOLUTION

The catastrophic events of the First World War had a fairly devastating effect on art and artistic design in general; jewellery was certainly no exception. After 1918 it seemed singularly inappropriate and passé to wear delicate diamond 'Garland' sprays while Art Nouveau naturalistic enamels seemed firmly rooted in a time obliterated in the trenches of the Western Front.

A sense of restlessness and change was quickly spreading through Britain, Europe and America and it was inevitable that this would be articulated in new and daring artistic forms and shapes in absolute contrast to all the established formulae of the past. Another vitally important change was the sense of freedom and independence gained by women in society. During the war women had worked alongside men and for the first time ever had become the principal breadwinners while their husbands were away fighting at the Front. It soon became apparent that the values and attitudes of life before the war when helpless, fluttering ladies were adorned from head to foot in formal jewels to reinforce the concept of feminine perfection were well and truly over. An altogether more mature, businesslike woman now emerged favouring simple, uncluttered clothes and jewellery which was both practical and utilitarian in concept and design.

Paris was still very much the epicentre of artistic inspiration and plans first proposed before the war were put into place to hold a major exhibition that could be a focal point for the diverse and often controversial ideas which were rapidly beginning to coalesce into one dominating style. In 1925 the rather grandly titled 'Exposition Internationale des Arts Décoratifs et Industriels Modernes' was opened in the centre of the city attracting several million visitors who came to admire furniture, sculpture, glass, ceramics, silver and particularly jewellery in which the principle common to all was 'new inspiration and real originality'. The exhibition made a huge cultural impact and gave its name to a movement which is synonymous today with elegance and chic – *Art Deco*.

Several different artistic concepts all contributed to Art Deco including Fauvism, Cubism and the early work of the Vienna Secessionists whose emphasis on minimal geometric lines was visibly apparent as far back as the start of the century. The simple, linear expression was quickly adopted by

Graduated Oriental pearl necklace on Art Deco diamond snap. In the 1920s natural pearls were prohibitively expensive. The market collapsed when cultured pearls were introduced by Kokichi Mikimoto

Group of Art Deco platinum, white gold, diamond and gem-set jewels made from 1925 to 1935.   Woolley & Wallis

fashionable couturiers such as Coco Chanel and Elsa Schiaparelli who both launched a range of elegant, tailored suits for daywear which were smart and comfortable, in large part due to their considerably shorter hemlines. Evening gowns in silk and satin were incredibly sophisticated and figure-hugging; the *gamine* look was in, accentuated by boyish figures and short, cropped hair. Unsurprisingly, long

diamond earrings and ropes of pearls and sautoirs were particularly popular at this time.

In 1922 Howard Carter discovered the tomb of the Egyptian boy king Tutankhamun. This inspired a host of Parisian jewellers such as Cartier, Van Cleef and La Cloche to create a range of 'Pharaonic' bracelets, brooches and clips set with solid clusters of emeralds, rubies, onyx and diamonds in a range of

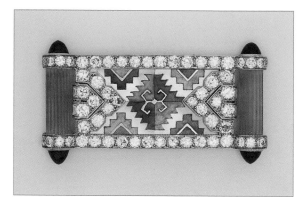

Unusual diamond, moonstone and sapphire plaque brooch c.1925 with an interesting mother-of-pearl marquetry pattern.

A pair of French onyx, coral and diamond stylised amphora drop earrings c.1925. Hancocks & Co

complex designs which included hieroglyphics, pyramids, scarabs and lotus flowers. This kind of jewellery is extremely rare today and commands staggeringly high prices at auction; a La Cloche or Cartier 'Egyptian' bracelet can easily fetch £150,000.

The idea of 'blocks' of colour strongly reinforced the Art Deco concept. Bold, decisive stones such as turquoise, chrysoprase, onyx and coral were cut into cubes, pyramids or batons and set against geometric clusters of 'white' diamonds which were mounted in 'architectural' three-dimensional platinum settings. Rock crystal was another important material. Inexpensive and plentiful, it could be cut and shaped into interesting angular shapes which looked

sensational when mounted with onyx and diamonds in jewellery which was strongly monochromatic in appearance.

Unlike Arts and Crafts jewellery, large costly precious gems were certainly back in fashion during the 1920s. Burmese rubies and sapphires and Colombian emeralds were polished into sleek geometric shapes such as rectangular step-cuts, triangles and squares which were placed in architectural frames totally devoid of unnecessary embellishment or fussy engraving. Diamonds were cut into a shape which is closely associated with Art Deco jewellery – the *baguette*. The baguette-cut was ideal for slotting into geometric frames and con-

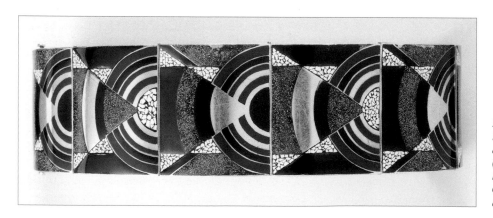

French silver, lacquered enamel and coquille d'oeuf *(eggshell) bracelet by Gustav and Gerard Sandoz c.1925.* John Jesse

A jade and diamond parure c.1925. This is attractively presented in the original fitted case, but note the rather mixed quality of the jade itself.

Bonhams/Bridgeman Art Library

Diamond and calibré cut emerald bow brooch c.1925.

trasted perfectly with similarly shaped *calibré*-cut emeralds, rubies and sapphires. Brilliant-cut diamonds had, by the late 1920s, completely lost their irregular cushion-like Victorian proportions and could be set in regular lines or clusters which also accentuated the architectural ideal.

The profound success of Art Deco jewellery between the wars consolidated the reputation and growth of several international houses, among the best known of which are Cartier, Boucheron and Van Cleef & Arpels. These jewellers each had their own distinctive 'house style.' Van Cleef, for example,

Three examples of Art Deco diamond and multi-gem set 'tutti frutti' jewels c.1930. The coloured stones probably originate from old Indian Mughal jewellery.
Hancocks & Co

pioneered the development of 'invisible settings' while Boucheron specialised in formal designs for the grand occasion and bold, angular jewels set with a combination of colourful hardstones in geometric formation. Cartier, probably the most famous jewellery house in the world today, constantly changed the direction of its output during the 1920s

and 1930s producing a remarkable diversity of superb designs inspired by the art of China, Persia, India and Egypt. For example, their range of 'tutti frutti' jewellery – bracelets, clips and collars – consisted of old Mughal gems (emeralds, rubies and sapphires) which had formerly adorned splendid turbans and neck ornaments. These gems, carved into the shape of flowers and leaves, were then remounted in platinum and diamond settings in a wide range of designs such as *jardinières,* charming vase of flowers studies which recall the pretty 'garden' jewels of the 18th century except that, instead of Georgian diamonds, the little pots and stems were invariably decorated with black lacquer or lines of calibré onyx or emeralds.

Diamond jardinière filled with an assemblage of carved hardstone flowers. The majority of these hardstones – chalcedony, nephrite and amethyst – are carved in Germany or Austria and may be stained in several different colours.

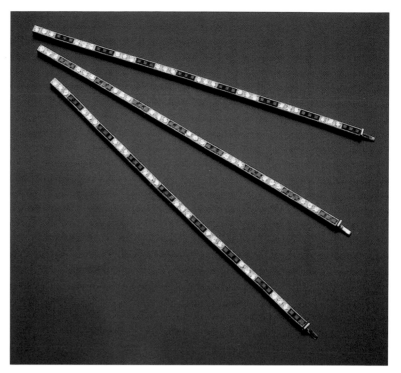

Cartier pavé diamond fob watch with matching brooch top c.1925.
Woolley & Wallis

Set of three platinum line bracelets set with diamonds and either rubies, emeralds or sapphires c.1925.
S. J. Phillips

Another important development was the expanding popularity of the wristwatch. From modest little gold or silver models by obscure Swiss manufacturers to fine diamond and precious gem-set examples by the big French houses, wristwatches had, by the early 1930s, totally superseded pocket watches. The angular shape of the watch head and bracelet were ideal for setting small brilliant and baguette-cut diamonds in geometric formation while less expensive models were attached to black or grey silk cordette straps. Many of these examples are surprisingly inexpensive today, although a well-known name such as Cartier, Patek Philippe or Rolex will impact considerably on value.

The 1920s were vintage years for the bracelet, from pretty, narrow, fully articulated ribbons with bow-shaped centrepieces to complex multi gem-set Egyptian Revival straps. Line bracelets were especially popular, composed of a simple row of brilliant or square-cut diamonds or diamonds in tandem with square onyx, emerald, ruby or sapphire. 1930s bracelets were altogether broader, heavier and

Emerald, onyx and diamond bracelet watch on a black leather strap c.1930.
Sandra Cronan

173

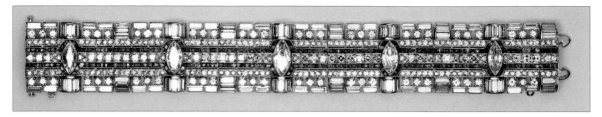

Broad platinum strap bracelet set with marquise, brilliant and baguette-cut diamonds together with channels of calibré-cut emeralds c.1935.

more angular; many of these later styles can be rather mixed in quality combining brilliant baguette and single-cut diamonds in repetitive scroll-like sections mounted in poorly finished white gold frames.

The brooch, in a myriad of interesting forms, was a consistent Art Deco favourite. In common with bracelets earlier, 1920s brooches still hung on to the softer, gentler forms of the Belle Époque era and, although designs in the latter part of the decade clearly anticipated the geometry of the 1930s, they are generally speaking prettier and more

This matching necklace and architectural pendant exhibit several characteristic themes associated with the Art Deco look: bold linear symmetry; the use of unusual contrasting materials (lapis lazuli, malachite and diamonds); engraved geometric patterns on the hardstone barrels and principal plaque. Hancocks & Co

imaginative. Sought-after designs included bows vividly contrasting diamonds with calibré-cut rubies or sapphires, epaulettes, fobs – usually articulated and set with small clusters of diamonds – ovals, cartouches, straps and hoops. Indeed, the hoop brooch was the quintessential Art Deco jewel composed of a large ring of onyx or rock crystal between diamond chevron sides. Novelties were also in fashion in the 1920s with sporting, racing and recreational subjects captured in gold or platinum. An interesting and fairly common method of wearing a simple brooch in the 1920s was the *sureté* or *jabot* pin in which the head of the jewel could be detached, the pin pushed through the garment and the head snapped back on the now-hidden shaft. Invariably fashioned as arrows or moulded glass buddhas, sureté pins are particularly collectable and relatively affordable today.

By the 1930s pretty pins and bows were superseded by all diamond-set architectural clips of which the most fashionable concept was the so-called double clip brooch. Composed of a pair of identical 'back-to-back' sections, each clip fastened on to a simple platinum or white gold frame. Superior models contained a series of tiny pegs which slotted into receiving apertures. Double clip brooches could therefore be worn as a single jewel or dismantled to be attached to both lapels of a smart jacket. The natural extension of the double clip was the plaque brooch where geometric clusters of brilliant-, baguette- and single-cut diamonds were fashioned into a simple oblong or cartouche. Plaque brooches were extremely common before the war and of highly variable quality.

The 1920s and 1930s will always be associated

An Art Deco paste double clip brooch c.1935. The pastes are painted with gold 'foil' on the backs to intensify their sparkle; note how badly the 'baguettes' fit into their settings.

Art Deco diamond double clip brooch set with brilliant and baguette-cut stones in geometric formation. Such clips could be dismantled from their frame for wearing on both lapels of a jacket. Woolley & Wallis

with glamour, excess, fantastic parties, dancing, film stars and riotous fun. Cigarette cases, the ultimate fashion accessory, ranged from straightforward nine carat gold or silver examples by Mappin & Webb or Asprey to highly colourful exotic creations by Cartier, La Cloche or Van Cleef & Arpels. These could be extraordinarily imaginative, decorated with enamel or set with hardstones such as lapis lazuli, jade and coral in a range of influences from Chinese

to Persian and Egyptian. Smoking was, of course, socially acceptable at this time and, in addition, both men and women habitually used cigarette holders in a range of materials which included amber, polished gold, onyx and hardstone with rose diamond fittings.

Women's accessories were in general use by the 1920s. Gold mesh evening bags were sometimes decorated with bold enamelling or set with lines of polished gems and diamonds while vanity cases in a

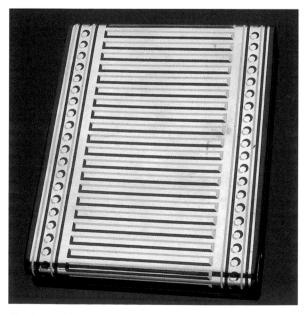

Cartier gold and enamel cigarette case c.1935. Quintessentially Art Deco in its linear composition, this example is almost radiator-like in inspiration.

Diamond pavé-set ribbon cluster brooch c.1930.
Sandra Cronan

(Left) Formal Art Deco sapphire, diamond and platinum necklace c.1935. Hancocks & Co

(Opposite) Typical group of Art Deco diamond jewellery mounted in platinum or white gold c.1930-1935.

(Below) Art Deco emerald and diamond strapwork bracelet c.1930. Sandra Cronan

variety of shapes and designs were frequently enamelled in pretty geometric patterns or coated in black lacquer. Sometimes these compacts were suspended from a tubular-shaped top section which doubled up as a lipstick holder – very messy at times when the contents leaked! Another highly fashionable accessory was the multi-purpose vanity case known as the *minaudière*. Patented by Van Cleef & Arpels, these useful receptacles contained compartments for cigarettes, powder, lipstick, comb, postage stamps and there was even space for a little watch head. Occasionally made from gold or silver and more commonly in white metal, French minaudières were sold in chic black suede wallets and perfectly complemented the sense of gaiety of the time.

Further reading

Christie's Twentieth Century Jewellery by Sally Everitt and David Lancaster (Pavilion Books Ltd.)

Antique and 20th Century Jewellery by Vivienne Becker (NAG Press)

Understanding Jewellery by David Bennett and Daniela Mascetti (Antique Collectors' Club)

SELECTED BIOGRAPHIES

ASHBEE, Charles Robert (1863-1942)
One of the leading exponents of the English Arts and Crafts movement. Ashbee founded the Guild of Handicraft in 1888 and became its chief designer, specialising in silver, enamel and gem-set necklaces, pendants and buckles of naturalistic inspiration such as peacocks, wild flowers and butterflies. In 1902 the Guild relocated from London to the Essex House Works in Chipping Campden, Gloucestershire, but closed in 1907 in the face of competition from Liberty & Co.

BOUCHERON, Frédéric (1830-1902)
French designer goldsmith specialising in fine diamond jewellery who founded his business on the Palais Royale in Paris in 1858. In 1893 he relocated to Place Vendôme where the firm operates successfully today. Regularly exhibiting in France and America. The firm is celebrated for its bold and innovative designs from striking Art Deco brooches to elegant and wearable naturalistic themes fashionable today.

BOULTON, Matthew (1728-1809)
An industrialist and steam engineer who in 1762 diversified part of his considerable business into the manufacture of faceted steel jewellery, accessories and buckles at his Soho works located at Snow Hill, Birmingham. In 1773 Boulton entered into an arrangement with Josiah Wedgwood to supply cut steel settings for neo-classical jasper cameos.

BROGDEN, John (active 1842-1885)
Designer goldsmith and retailer based at Henrietta Street, Covent Garden. Brogden specialised in several contrasting styles but is probably best known for the manufacture of architectural, classical and Assyrian-inspired jewellery using bright yellow gold, hardstone cameos, enamel and pyrope garnet. His signature is JB in capitals in an oval cartouche.

BROWN, William (1748-1825)
 and **Charles (1749-1795)**
Gem engravers specialising in neo-classical profiles who both exhibited at the Royal Academy.

BULGARI
Italian jewellery dynasty founded by Sotirio Bulgari in 1879 in Rome and subsequently located to the Via dei Condotti in 1905. Bulgari has been one of the most successful international jewellery retailers since the 1960s specialising in a combination of top of the range special commissions and versatile easy-to-wear day jewels mounted with bold and colourful semi-precious polished gems or ancient coins.

BURCH, Edward (1730-1814)
Sculptor, gem engraver and Royal Academician who worked for both Josiah Wedgwood and James Tassie specialising in technically accomplished classical profiles.

BURGES, William (1827-1881)
Architect, designer and all-round polymath, much of Burges' output exhibited a strong Gothic Revivalist influence such as a fine gold pectoral cross and chain forming part of the Hull Grundy Collection at the British Museum and the jewellery made for the wedding of his patron, the Marquis of Bute.

CARTIER
From its foundation in Paris in 1847, the name Cartier has been synonymous with superb jewellery, accessories, wristwatches and objets d'art. Established by Louis-François Cartier (1819-1904), the firm was subsequently taken over and expanded by his three grandsons Louis, Jacques and Pierre, each with responsibility for operating the salons located respectively in Paris, London and New York.

Cartier has never compromised the quality of its materials or the originality and execution of its designs. The firm was among the first to use platinum in intricate 'Belle Époque' diamond garland settings and by the 1920s and 1930s it was selling the finest jewels and accessories inspired by the art of India, Persia, the Orient, Ancient Egypt and Russia to many of the world's most celebrated and distinguished clients.

CASTELLANI, Fortunato Pio (1793-1865)

Italian goldsmith and one of the leading interpreters of jewellery in the archaeological taste. Castellani mastered the skill of applying gold granular decoration on to many of his classical designs. This made a huge impact since the technique was thought to have been lost with the ancient Etruscans. To reinforce the integrity of the classical statement, he made extensive use of ancient coins, hardstone intaglios and scarabs in settings which took the form of amphoras, fibulas and *bullae,* a form of round ancient amulet. On Castellani's death, the business was continued by his sons Alessandro (1824-1883) and Augusto (1829-1914). The firm's mark is two overlapping letter 'Cs' in back to back formation.

CHILD & CHILD (active 1891-1915)

A firm of London silversmiths and jewellers owned by Walter and Harold Child specialising in attractive and reasonably priced gold, silver and silver gilt jewels such as pendants, brooches and buckles. Recognisable for their stylised wing shapes, many of these pieces were translucent enamelled in turquoise blue and green and were sold in distinctive green leather cases. Their mark was a sunflower with the monogram 'CC'.

COOPER, John Paul (1869-1933)

Arts and Crafts designer goldsmith who trained under Henry Wilson. After becoming head of metalwork at the Birmingham School of Art he left to start his own business. Using his favoured medium of fifteen carat gold, John Paul Cooper soon mastered the technique of cloisonné and champlevé enamelling and produced hundreds of items of jewellery and accessories set with coloured gems or a range of unusual organic materials. Much of his output was heavily influenced by the work of Henry Wilson.

DUNLOP, Sibyl (1889-1968)

Scottish born Arts and Crafts designer and retailer who trained in Brussels and opened a shop in Kensington Church Street specialising in silver jewellery mounted with gems and hardstones in characteristically understated colours. The fact that many of her designs involved gems set in naturalistic and geometric cluster formation led to frequent confusion with the very similar work of another jeweller, Dorrie Nossiter.

FABERGÉ, Peter Carl (1846-1920)

Unrivalled Russian designer goldsmith. After serving an apprenticeship in Frankfurt and visiting several European cities, Fabergé returned to Russia and in 1870 took over control of the family business. In 1882 the firm showed at the Moscow Pan Russian Exhibition where it won the Gold Medal. His reputation spread rapidly and in 1884 Tsar Alexander III commissioned the first Imperial Easter egg designed in plain white enamel and opening to reveal a 'surprise' – a miniature gold hen containing a jewelled crown within its body. In the same year Fabergé was awarded the Royal Warrant. Imperial patronage sealed his success and he won important commissions from diverse distinguished customers including several European and Oriental ruling families. Apart from shops in four Russian cities, he opened a salon in London's Bond Street selling his incomparable jewels, accessories and 'objects of fantasy'. The war years saw a gradual decline in Fabergé's fortunes and the firm was ultimately closed down by the Bolsheviks in 1918. Fabergé managed to escape to Lausanne where he died in 1920.

Fabergé's phenomenal success was in no small part down to his decision to expand his business from the manufacture of purely functional items to the production of decorative and ornamental objets d'art embracing a broad range of exquisite articles such as hardstone carvings, flower studies in rock crystal pots and, of course, the fifty-seven Imperial Easter eggs. He employed a team of highly skilled workmasters, each with their own particular speciality. Fabergé's use of translucent enamel and gold applied in several different colours was simply incomparable, combining supreme good taste with flawless attention to detail and technical mastery of the medium. His association with the Imperial Family simply adds to the potency of the Fabergé legend.

FAHRNER, Theodor (1868-1929)

German jewellery designer who anticipated the geometric, linear forms of the Art Deco period with his range of 'Affordable Art Jewellery' in silver, enamel and panels of hardstone set in borders of marcasite.

FALIZE, Alexis (1811-1898)
and his son Lucien (1838-1898)

specialised in highly colourful cloisonné enamel jewellery of Japanese and Persian inspiration such as their range of flat disc-shaped pendants depicting Oriental birds and flowers.

FOUQUET, Georges (1862-1957)

Art Nouveau goldsmith celebrated for his bold and powerful designs incorporating diamonds, gems and plique-à-jour enamel. His best known work was a fabulous enamel snake bracelet designed by Alphonse Mucha for the actress Sarah Bernhardt.

FROMENT-MEURICE, François-Désirée (1802-1855)

Parisian jeweller who pioneered designs inspired by Gothic and Renaissance art known as the *style Cathédrale*.

GASKIN, Arthur (1862-1928)
and his wife Georgina (1866-1934)

Goldsmiths and silversmiths producing exceptional Arts and Crafts silver and gem-set jewellery. Closely associated with William Morris and the Pre-Raphaelites, Gaskin jewellery is strongly naturalistic favouring colourful clusters of cabochon-cut gems in leaf and tendril settings.

GIULIANO, Carlo (1831-1895)

Leading figure in 19th century Classical and Renaissance Revivalist jewellery celebrated for his accomplished use of enamel. Born in Naples, Giuliano served his apprenticeship with Castellani before setting up a workshop in London and his own retail premises in Piccadilly in 1874. His 'art jewellery' is notable for its originality and under-stated elegance, using subtle gemstones such as tourmaline, zircon, hessonite, garnet and Ceylon sapphire which blended together extremely well in compatible gold settings, and were embellished with intricate enamelling and often further enamelled and engraved on the backs.

After his death the business was continued by his two sons, Carlo and Arthur, who designed equally distinctive jewels such as necklaces, bracelets and brooches characteristic for their use of monochrome enamel. Carlo Giuliano's mark is the monogram 'CG' in an oval cartouche and 'C & AG' after 1896.

GRIMA, Andrew (born 1921)

Contemporary jeweller and craftsman using bold and unusual uncut crystals or coloured gems such as aquamarine, topaz and pink beryl in striking textured gold mounts. Grima pioneered daring abstract forms in the 1960s and 1970s and his work is highly collectable today. His signature is 'Grima' or 'AG.'

HORNER, Charles Henry (1870-1949)

Early 20th century Halifax silversmith producing in-expensive but strongly defined enamel and silver jewellery, especially pendants, brooches and hatpins in naturalistic and Celtic themes. His monogram 'CH' is invariably accompanied by a Chester Assay Office hallmark.

JENSEN, Georg (1866-1935)

Danish silversmith and goldsmith well known for striking and wearable jewellery largely inspired by nature defined in sculptured, semi-abstract forms. Jensen's sound business acumen and marketing skills has meant that the firm flourishes successfully today. Designs are individually numbered, include gold as well as silver and sometimes incorporate polished gems and hardstones such as lapis lazuli, moonstone and garnet. Pieces are signed in full or the monogram 'GJ' in a circle of dots.

KNOX, Archibald (1864-1933)

Goldsmith, silversmith and designer of Arts and Crafts jewellery. He produced numerous designs for Liberty & Co bearing a strong Celtic influence decorated with enamel and set with gems typical of the genre such as opal, moonstone, turquoise and blister pearl in what became known as the Liberty 'Cymric' range.

KUTCHINSKY (established 1893)

London based jewellers active today and prominent in the 1960s and 1970s for fine diamond jewellery including abstract gold pieces set with interesting combinations of gemstones and pendants mounted with discs of hardstone such as malachite and tiger's eye.

LALIQUE, René (1860-1945)

Renowned Parisian goldsmith with incomparable technique and a gifted imagination. One of the leading representatives of the Art Nouveau movement which spread through Europe at the end of the 19th century, Lalique created visionary jewels in gold, silver and even unusual metals such as aluminium, many of which were decorated with plique-à-jour enamel, fine coloured gems or moulded glass plaques. Lalique's appreciation and application of the natural form was represented by many intriguing and evocative themes which combined several contrasting motifs within the single jewel such as insects, flowers – both flourishing and decaying – and the female nude figure. The overall effect was unfailingly sensuous, harmonious and fantastic.

LIBERTY & CO

Founded by Arthur Lasenby Liberty (1843-1917), Liberty & Co of Regent Street, London championed the cause of the Arts and Crafts movement by commissioning several of its leading designers such as Archibald Knox, Arthur Gaskin and Jessie M. King to produce affordable and wearable jewels for the firm's 'Cymric' range. The commercial needs of the company were incompatible with the artistic integrity of C.R. Ashbee, however, but Liberty was crucial to the development of Art jewellery in England, bringing the work of small individual craftsmen to the attention of the wider public.

MARCHANT, Nathaniel (1739-1816)

Gem engraver who enjoyed considerable success in his lifetime carrying out commissions for many prominent families and politicians such as William Pitt and Earl Spencer.

MELILLO, Giacinto (1846-1915)

Gifted Neapolitan goldsmith who took over the running of Castellani's workshop in 1870. Heavily influenced by classical and 'archaeological' themes, Melillo is probably best known for his Etruscan-style gold jewellery fashioned as winged cherubs, lions and cornucopias decorated with minute granulation and twisted wirework.

MURPHY, Henry George (1884-1939)

Harry Murphy trained under Henry Wilson as a silversmith and goldsmith where he gained considerable experience working with metals and decorative enamel. After a period spent in Berlin with Emil Lettré, he returned to England and set up his own shop in Weymouth Street, London, known as the Falcon Studio. Murphy was an accomplished draughtsman and designer in several diverse media and his output exhibits a range of influences from Gothic and Renaissance to Art Deco. He was also a gifted teacher. His signature, 'HGM', is accompanied by a falcon crest.

MURRLE BENNETT & CO
(active 1884-1914)

Firm of goldsmiths and silversmiths founded by Ernest Murrle, a German-born jeweller who entered into partnership with a Mr Bennett in 1884. Creative in the Arts and Crafts medium, the firm worked closely with Arthur Liberty who offered an ideal shop window for the company's elegant and wearable necklaces, brooches and pendants frequently set with blister pearls and semi-precious stones such as turquoise matrix. The firm's signature is 'MB' or 'MB & Co.'

OVED, Mosheh (active 1903-1953)

Founder of Cameo Corner, the celebrated Bloomsbury antique jewellers, Mosheh Oved was a near-penniless Polish Jew who, on arriving in London, persevered to build up an incomparable stock of rare jewels and a list of clients which included Queen Mary and Rudolph Valentino. Together with his common-law wife, Sah, he also designed and made a range of silver and gold rings fashioned into the shape of animals and birds notable for their sensitivity.

PHILLIPS, Robert (1810-1881)

'Phillips of Cockspur Street' was established in 1846 and specialised in the manufacture of archaeological and Renaissance revival jewellery embellished with fine enamel and compatible gems in high quality gold settings such as coral fringe necklaces, intricate enamel pendants and Assyrian-style diadems. Phillips was also important for his early encourage-ment and sponsorship of Carlo Giuliano. Upon the death of Robert Phillips, the business was continued by his son Alfred. Their jewellery is marked with a stylised Prince of Wales feather in a lozenge border.

PICHLER, Giovanni (1734-1791)
and half brother Luigi (1773-1854)

Italian gem engravers specialising in fine inter-pretations of classical subjects and profiles which are sometimes found in late 18th century hardstone rings and necklaces. Their signature was inscribed in Greek capitals.

PINCHBECK, Christopher (1672-1732)

Fleet Street watchmaker who perfected the tech-nique of combining an alloy of copper and zinc to produce a versatile metal which successfully imitated gold. The material should not be confused with cheaper and inferior gilt metal of later manufacture.

RAMSDEN & CARR

Omar Ramsden (1873-1939) and Alwyn Carr (1872-1940) were leading figures of the English Arts and Crafts movement. After meeting at the Sheffield School of Art, they subsequently formed a successful partnership in London from 1898-1919 producing silverware, silver jewellery and enamels.

SAULINI, Tommaso (1793-1864)
and his son Luigi (1819-1883)

Italian hardstone and shell cameo engravers and portrait sculptors notable for the fine detail and accuracy of their work, much of which was signed T. Saulini F. or L. Saulini F.

STREETER, Edwin (1834-1923)

An important figure in the late Victorian London retail jewellery sector, Edwin Streeter was an excavator and dealer in gems from around the world who set up in business in Conduit Street in 1867 and subsequently in Bond Street. He produced regular colour catalogues of his stock which today give us a better understanding of original prices and what was fashionable in the 1890s.

TASSIE, James (1735-1799)

Scottish discoverer of a technique in which real hardstone cameos and intaglios were cast and faith-fully copied in paste glass. Using a sulphur based mould, Tassie produced a compound which could be coloured or colourless and transparent or opaque. They were enormously popular in the 1770s; indeed a set of several thousands was commissioned by the Empress of Russia.

TIFFANY, Charles Lewis (1812-1902)
and Louis Comfort (1848-1933)

Leading American jewellery designers and retailers. After initial success in the stationery and giftware business, C.L. Tiffany diversified into the design and manufacture of jewellery and silver first in New York and subsequently in Paris and London. Adept in a broad range of fine and applied arts, the firm has consistently produced elegant jewellery whether in the Belle Époque 'Garland' taste, Art Nouveau and Deco or Post War and Modernist styles. Today, Tiffany & Co is one of the world's leading brand names for up-to-the-minute gold and silver jewellery and giftware.

VAN CLEEF & ARPELS

A leading firm of French jewellery designers and manufacturers active since 1898 when the firm was founded by Alfred Van Cleef and his two brothers-in-law Charles and Julien Arpels. Among their most successful accomplishments was the technique of 'invisibly setting' gems such as rubies and sapphires into striking platinum and gold jewellery such as the petals of flower spray brooches. The firm is internationally known today for its distinctive jewellery, wristwatches, accessories and perfumes.

VEVER MAISON

Founded by Paul Vever in 1821 and continued by his two sons Paul (1851-1915) and Henri (1854-1942), Maison Vever produced elegant and often understated Art Nouveau gold and enamel jewellery. Henri was also the author of a definitive three-volume history of French 19th century jewellery.

WIESE, Jules (1818-1890)
and his son Louis (1852-1923)

The Wieses have gained particular recognition in recent years for their distinctive and faithful interpretation of jewellery in the Gothic taste. Jules trained in the Froment-Meurice workshops before establishing his own business in 1865. The firm used simple polished cabochons of gems such as ruby and Ceylon sapphire as well as ancient coins in mounts which were hammered and left intentionally simplistic to suggest a medieval appearance. The signature, occasionally used, was JW with a star above.

WILSON, Henry (1864-1934)

Important figurehead of English Arts and Crafts jewellery, both as an innovative designer and a mentor to other goldsmiths such as Harry Murphy and John Paul Cooper. Wilson taught at the Central School and Royal College of Arts and was strongly influenced by medieval and ecclesiastical imagery. Much of his work was decorated with colourful enamel, such as his celebrated 'Diana' tiara studded with gems and cylinders of rock crystal.

WINSTON, Harry (1896-1978)

New York entrepreneurial jeweller. The key to Harry Winston's phenomenal success was to buy 'unfashionable' estate jewellery, break out the stones and remodel them into new and stylish settings which gained immediate popularity with a wealthy New York and international clientele. The appositely named 'King of Diamonds' handled many of the rarest and most important diamonds and precious gems during his lifetime, even donating incomparable stones such as the Hope Diamond to the Smithsonian Institute in Washington.

A turn of the century tiara set with diamonds, bouton pearls and a gallery of graduated drop shape pearls of singular colour, purity and consistency. Hancocks & Co.

Jewellery Compendium

1. VALUATIONS

Valuations can be a highly subjective matter where assessments vary considerably depending upon the type of item involved, its rarity, design and composition and even the location where it is examined. Unfortunately, not all valuers are as experienced as others which is why it is important to employ the services of a qualified specialist with a proven track record who has handled similar jewellery to your own. In my opinion, there is absolutely no point in taking a Fabergé frame or Boucheron bracelet to a high street jeweller selling modern manufactured gold, watches and giftware while many auction houses are surprisingly ill-equipped to advise accurate, up-to-date values on fine and rare diamonds, objets d'art and antique jewels.

Jewellery valuers in the U.K. are encouraged to undertake a two year diploma course in Gemmology ultimately gaining fellowship of the Gemmological Association (F.G.A.). A further year's study of diamonds leads to the Gem Diamond Diploma (D.G.A.). A large number of leading shops are also affiliated to the National Association of Goldsmiths (N.A.G.) which provides in-depth courses and seminars for its members, teaching the essentials of good valuation practice as well as much of the technical data necessary to do their job properly.

In an increasingly litigious world, the importance of a detailed, comprehensive valuation with accompanying digital photography cannot be overstated. A document which states accurate grading of diamonds, country of origin, quality and authenticity of coloured gems, the age of antique jewels and diverse aspects of weight, condition, repairs and defects will not only enable you to replace a loss with another item as near to the original as possible but may also help to prove legal title in the event of recovery.

What Type of Valuation Do I Need?

The majority of jewellery valuations are provided for insurance purposes. Generally speaking, this involves theoretical replacement of a loss in the retail sector with an item of equivalent design, quality and value to the original. A piece of jewellery purchased, say, at Cartier or Tiffany & Co will undoubtedly have a different 'mark-up' from another bought from a dealer in 'the Trade' which is why it is crucial to establish precisely where any replacement would take place. Similarly, certain types of antique jewellery – Castellani, Lalique or Fabergé for example – may only be available from highly specialised shops and dealers in the London West End sector or even overseas, underlining once again the importance of getting professional advice from the right people.

Probate valuations are provided upon goods which form part of the estate of a deceased person and are based upon the price which the item might reasonably be expected to fetch if sold on the open market at time of death. Open Market values correspond to the price the item would be likely to fetch at auction and are thus lower than retail insurance levels. Other types of valuation include Capital Gains Tax, Family Division and Divorce (sometimes rather acrimonious with a degree of tact and diplomacy recommended). Post Loss Assessment is provided as a retrospective opinion for items lost but where no previous valuation may exist.

How Much Should I Pay?

Some valuers still calculate their charges based upon a set percentage of the total value of their customer's property. Personally, I believe this method is somewhat unethical and may be open to abuse; also, there is always the question hanging in the air that assessment has been made on the high side to obtain a bigger fee. The fair and proper approach adopted by the majority of shops, valuers and auction houses today is to levy a fee according to how long it takes to do the job. This is usually a set hourly rate plus VAT and may involve an additional expense for subsequent research. Whichever method is used, do establish at the outset a formal charging structure as well as the credentials of the valuer.

2. FAKES, FORGERIES AND ENHANCEMENTS

Jewellery, just like every other artistic endeavour, has suffered more than its fair share of faking and forgery. The problem is not a recent one either. From early times brass and gilded metal have masqueraded as gold while glass and imitation stones have been effective substitutes for diamonds and precious gems for centuries. Jewellery panders to the very worst of man's baser instincts adding spice and intrigue to the more prosaic attractions on offer. Greed is a very potent ingredient in the myth of jewellery, often resulting in conflict and financial calamity. Here is a list, by no means exhaustive, of some of the more common pitfalls encountered on a regular basis in the world of gems and jewellery.

(i) *Gems.* It is possible today to synthesise, enhance, radiate, improve and alter the appearance of practically every species of gem in the world today. Diamonds are imitated by a whole range of colourless gems, some crude and obvious and others technically outstanding. Flawed diamonds are sometimes lasered to remove carbon defects while fancy coloured diamonds can be enhanced to change or intensify colour. When purchasing a diamond, do ensure it is accompanied by a certificate from a leading international laboratory to establish authenticity. A looming problem for the jewellery industry in the next ten years is cultured diamonds. These are just about as good as they get and it is only a matter of time before unscrupulous merchants start to pass them off as genuine. To counteract the dilemma and boost buyers' confidence, diamond polishers have started to laser tiny serial numbers on to the girdles of their stones which can then be compared with a formal certificate.

Rubies and sapphires have been synthesised since the 1920s and many Art Deco jewels are set with these man-made gems. View any calibré or baton-cut gems with suspicion, especially when set in cocktail watches, bracelets and clips. In the same way, ensure

that any modern rubies and sapphires purchased in the Far East are accompanied by an independent certificate of authenticity.

Of all precious gems, emerald is probably the one which has been the most extensively enhanced; indeed, the situation has become so bad that the emerald market has visibly deteriorated in recent years. A certificate is therefore essential, particularly for modern emeralds of 'good' colour.

Opals are enhanced and strengthened in colour by cementing layers above and below the genuine material known as either doublets or triplets.

Aquamarines are imitated by synthetic blue spinels while cheap colour changing synthetic corundums have been sold as valuable alexandrite since the 1950s.

Glass has been an effective substitute for costly gems since the Middle Ages. Glass – or paste – is softer than real gemstones, indicated by abrasions and 'moulded' facets on the surface. Often containing bubbles and swirls, glass is a poor conductor of heat and is therefore warm to the touch. Eighteenth century paste jewellery can be remarkably deceptive, so close inspection of Georgian rings and brooches is recommended. Finally, do examine foil-backed stones – particularly sapphire, ruby and pink topaz – with great care. Your precious ruby might just be foiled rock crystal.

(ii) *Jewellery.* Treat all 'signed' jewellery with a measured degree of caution. The exploitation of fake Fabergé has become so widespread as to give rise to the term 'Fauxbergé'. Similarly, all the well-known names – Cartier, Van Cleef & Arpels, Tiffany and Bulgari – have all been extensively faked. Some of these are so downright awful that the signatures are spelt incorrectly.

Fake 'signed' jewels – and indeed fake period jewellery in general – always lack the quality, patina and integrity of their genuine counterparts. Settings are badly finished while gems are inferior and diamonds are often flawed. Much of the 'Art Deco' style jewellery sold today is made in the Far East to a superior standard, but the diamonds are perfectly proportioned modern cuts and the coloured gems exhibit a machine-like consistency. Nineteenth century revivalist jewellery is both faked in its entirety and is forged by adding a spurious signature to the setting. A false Castellani or Giuliano cartouche is usually crude and soft-soldered in lead but superior examples have fooled many.

The quality of much contemporary plique-à-jour enamel is extremely good resulting in some exceptionally clever 'Art Nouveau' fakes such as butterflies and figurative brooches. If in doubt, check with an expert in the field.

Eighteenth century and early 19th century jewellery is particularly desirable today which means that plenty of fakes abound. Watch out for 'Georgian' gold belcher link muff chains – the modern copies are heavier and not so delicate as the originals. Other 'Regency' fakes include twin heart rings, Giardinetti rings, rose diamond earrings in settings which are just too crisp to be original and message jewellery such as 'regard' rings and lockets.

(iii) *Wristwatches*. Wristwatches are probably faked more comprehensively than just about any other commodity in the luxury goods market and the better the name, the more likely the fake. Manufacturers such as Cartier and Rolex are constantly on their guard for fake copies of Tank watches and Oyster Chronometers and we have all seen those amazing pictures of phoney watches being crushed under a steamroller. Always ensure you purchase a watch from a totally reliable source and check it is supplied with the original box and guarantee.

Finally, as a general rule of thumb do check the sales ticket carefully. Fakes and forgeries are usually sold at prices which are by no means cheap but which are just too good to be true if the article were genuine. Always obtain a receipt which gives a clear and unequivocal statement of age and origin. If buying from an auction house the same rule applies, although it is wise to bear in mind the well-known phrase used extensively in this business – *caveat emptor* – buyer beware.

3. CLEANING, RESTORATION AND REPAIRS

A clumsy and crude repair to a good quality antique jewel will ruin its integrity and may seriously affect its value. The problem is not so widespread nowadays, probably because jewellers and their customers have a greater awareness of the importance of prime condition, in which repairs and conversions are only undertaken as a last resort. Nevertheless, 'historical'

(Above) 18th century diamond brooch.

(Above right) The back of the same brooch showing an appalling hotchpotch of bungled repairs.

modifications are depressingly commonplace in which original fittings, pins and loops have been removed, makers' marks deleted, hallmarks chopped out of Victorian rings, roller catches attached to antique brooches, ill-matching gems and modern diamonds insensitively set in antique frames and, last but certainly not least, ugly lead solder used in place of discreet gold.

The fact of the matter is that regardless of how skilled the repair or conversion, an experienced valuer can always tell. So, unless you intend to keep the piece 'in the family' for perpetuity, give the matter considerable thought first. Buyers of antique jewellery are just like buyers of old paintings, ceramics and furniture. They want material which is untouched, preferably unrestored and which last saw the inside of a jewellers on the day of original purchase.

Having said all that, there is no point in locking your brooch or bracelet away in a drawer unworn and neglected for years simply because it is unfashionable and difficult to wear. The key is to seek the right advice from a qualified jeweller and preferably one with an excellent local reputation. A good starting point is to check that the shop is a member of the National Association of Goldsmiths (N.A.G.). This means that you have recourse to a higher authority – a kind of 'jewellery ombudsman' – should you be dissatisfied with the service you receive.

Many well-established jewellers, particularly in Central London, are not affiliated to the N.A.G. but still offer excellent workshop facilities. It is usually worthwhile checking with B.A.D.A. (the British Antique Dealers' Association) or L.A.P.A.D.A. (the Association of Art and Antique Dealers) for a list of current members.

Jewellery repairs and conversions can be extremely expensive so do ensure that you obtain a written estimate before the work takes place. No matter how competent the jeweller, some aspects of restoration work are inadvisable. Examples include rare works of art such as Fabergé, early jewellery, enamel, gold filigree and mosaics. Nevertheless, some modifications may actually enhance value. These include converting small uncommercial Victorian cluster brooches into necklace clasps, polishing the worn and abraded surfaces on antique coloured gems, refoiling period gems where the original tinfoil has deteriorated and replacing discoloured and unsightly pearls and turquoises with new specimens which match the originals.

Cleaning

Just like repairs, cleaning should be approached with great care. Many antique gems and jewels should only be handled by experienced restorers while pearls are especially vulnerable. Nevertheless, you can make a huge difference to the appearance of your own gold and silver jewellery – and rings in particular – by soaking an old toothbrush in warm water, applying a few drops of washing-up liquid and gently brushing behind and around the setting with small circular motions to dislodge dust and dirt. Avoid soap which dries to leave white deposits and dry thoroughly with kitchen paper. This method is excellent for diamonds, rubies, sapphires and semi-precious dress rings such as aquamarine, citrine and amethyst in open back settings. It is unsuitable for porous or fragile gems such as emerald, pearl, opal and turquoise. One last point – put the plug in the sink!

INDEX